Blue Sky Project Management

Blue Sky Project Management

How 21st Century Innovation Gets To Market

John R. Maculley, Jr., MBA, PMP

Printed in the United States of America

(ISBN 10) 1-4196-9056-6

(ISBN 13) 978-1-419-69056-3

"Any intelligent fool can make things bigger and more complex... it takes a touch of genius - and a lot of courage to move in the opposite direction."

- Albert Einstein

Contents

Preface

Based on nearly two decades of experience working on some of the most innovative projects the world has to offer, John R. Maculley, Jr., argues in favor of measuring project performance by the rate-of-learning occurring within the project team, rather than by arbitrary time-based completion percentages not tied to the innovation. Mr. Maculley honed his unique approach to project management while working with a multitude of benchmark organizations. For example, as part of GE's Advanced Programs Department, he helped to develop a 21st century military fighter jet engine prototype composed of ceramic airfoils and carbon matrix composite housings. While working with Boeing's Commercial Aircraft Division, Mr. Maculley helped to develop the Boeing 717, one of the world's first jetliners designed using a full-scale digital 3-D solid model prototype. He also worked with NASA's Academy of Program, Project, and Engineering Leadership (APPEL) and NASA's Engineering and Safety Center (NESC) to help develop knowledge management strategies and communications portals currently in use across the Agency. Mr. Maculley now splits his time between the corporate world and academia. He serves as a research and development program manager at Micron Technology, a leading semiconductor company with a patent portfolio thought to be more powerful than that of Intel, Hewlett Packard, IBM, and Microsoft. Mr. Maculley also serves as a university instructor for both Boise State University and University of Phoenix. He teaches undergraduate and graduate-level business courses on project management, product development, marketing, quality management, and operations management. Using his extensive experience in new product development, Mr. Maculley developed a proven model to bring the most innovative *Blue Sky* projects to market successfully.

Blue Sky Project Management provides a systematic approach to managing innovation projects according to their unique characteristics. In this frame-changing book, Mr. Maculley presents a step-by-step methodology that is easy understand and simple to follow. Using flow-diagrams to explain each step of the process, he introduces unique templates to aid even the most non-project oriented organizations in accomplishing their goals. Starting with a vision of innovation, he will guide both project managers and corporate executives alike through the process of connecting strategy to operations, developing a portfolio of strategic innovation projects, and managing each one in such a way that innovation and performance are maximized, while bureaucracy and inefficient overhead are minimized. Scientists and engineers will feel empowered by this tailored approach to project management, rather than experiencing feelings of frustration and micro-management under the confines of more traditional methodologies.

Although *Blue Sky Project Management* was written specifically for the management of innovation projects, it is also a great resource for all 21st century thinkers with great ideas and the desire to see them fulfilled.

In Gratitude

Dedicated to Colonel John E. "Johnny" Cormier (USAF Retired)

Even before I married his grand-daughter in 1992, within the plain white walls of the Chapel of the Centurion – a historic building positioned inside the moat of Fort Monroe, John Cormier was busy planting the seeds of project management. He often expounded on the virtues of project management, as both a noble profession and a worthwhile endeavor to focus one's life. Over the years, we have enjoyed many conversations, exchanging opinions on fine wines, business strategies, leadership, faith, family, and project management. Through these stimulating conversations, I have learned that our lives are much like innovation projects - chock full of uncertainty and risk - if they are well managed, everyone benefits. In this life we are all project managers.

John R. Maculley, Jr.
Boise, Idaho
Spring 2008

Introduction

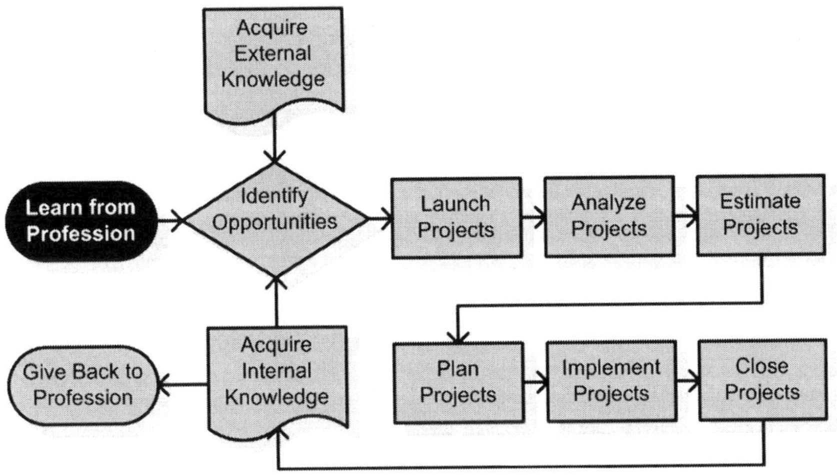

Why We Need a New Methodology

Innovation is difficult to manage and easy to suffocate. This dilemma may be obvious to anyone who has worked in research and development, yet it nevertheless remains unresolved by those who need the solution most. Innovation cannot be forced or demanded, but rather must be encouraged and nurtured. For innovation to flourish, the right environment must be established. Similar to an innovation ecosystem, workplaces must be designed to foster the growth of good ideas. Taking into account office design, meeting spaces, and team proximity are important when creating an environment of innovation. A proper workplace structure will help innovation thrive, but too much bureaucracy will kill it dead. It can be argued that managing innovation well is one of the most important business challenges we face in the 21st century, but why is this enigma, called innovation, so different?

Innovation requires bringing new ideas to market where little prior data is available. It's charting new ground and exploring new frameworks of thought. Most management methodologies currently in use to manage innovation are either too simple to capture the complexity of a disruptive technology, or overly bureaucratic, thereby squashing the innovation before it comes to life. We need a methodology that can handle the intricacies of bringing innovations to market quickly, with reduced risk, and controlled costs. Innovation requires a new approach to this very old problem.

What's Different About the *Blue Sky* Method?

There are three key focus areas that enable managers to maintain project control at a macro level, while not controlling the activities of the subject-matter experts. First, is the alignment of the innovation with the strategy of the organization. This should be the primary focus of the executive team during the opportunity identification stage. It makes no sense to innovate for the sake of innovating, but rather innovating to solve a clearly understood and worthwhile problem in the marketplace. Companies that lack a clear focus tend to fall into this trap. When a company lacks focus, they tend to concentrate on cost reduction initiatives. Their business processes are typically inefficient and overly complex. Innovation companies need to differentiate themselves in the marketplace by chartering new ground. Coming to market with a me-too product or service is not going to provide the kind of advantages required to sustain corporate growth. The driver of innovation should be based on making profits as quickly as possible, otherwise the effort is reduced to a mere academic exercise. It's also important to understand the intended market for the innovation and ensure the organization that is funding the project has intentions of entering that market-space in a meaningful way. Chapter 2 will describe several methods of aligning innovation with corporate strategy.

Second, is the management of risk. Innovation projects, by definition, are more risky than standard enhancement type projects, where the outcome is more predictable. This characteristic of high risk is often the main element of concern when cancelling highly innovative projects before they have proven their worth. Executives not comfortable with uncertainty often kill projects they feel they can't control. To overcome this issue, the *Blue Sky* method of project management focuses heavily on risk management throughout the entire project lifecycle. NASA is one of the leaders in the area of risk management and their proven techniques and templates will be introduced in Chapter 4.

Finally, managers must focus on knowledge management while the project is in progress, but most importantly after the project has been implemented. This is one of the most important continuous improvement activities a company can undertake, yet is often overlooked as project teams look for the next exciting challenge to take on. Simply emailing a few lessons-learned after a project wraps up will not be sufficient for most innovation teams to improve. A full-scale communications strategy is required to ensure knowledge is transferred from one project team to the next. Chapter 9 will introduce the power of knowledge management and several 21st century approaches to sharing information cross-functionally.

Who Benefits From The *Blue Sky* Method?

There are many great methodologies for project management in the world, however, most are designed for either the construction or software industries. They have little emphasis on projects that have an unknown set of steps required to accomplish highly ambiguous outcomes. Unfortunately, traditional project management methodologies fall short when applied to innovation projects where managing the learning-cycle is more important than managing the discrete task. Innovative companies wanting to implement new strategies would have a difficult time following the traditional project management methodologies prescribed by most management consulting firms - methods heavily weighted on documentation. Furthermore, research and development organizations wanting to bring disruptive technologies to market would quickly become frustrated by most project management methodologies requiring a fully developed work breakdown structure (WBS) and other detailed documentation. Scientists typically don't know how they will solve a problem until they begin the process. This iterative approach to innovation often causes conflict with traditional approaches to project management. Micron Technology, one of the world's leading developers of high-end semiconductor products, has developed the most powerful patent portfolio in the world, ahead of giants like IBM, Intel, Hewlett Packard, and Microsoft. To accomplish this tremendous pace of innovation, Micron focuses on rapidly scaling the learning-curve, rather than micro managing the minutia.

Research and development organizations can certainly benefit by implementing a new project management methodology, however it could also be argued that anyone with a fresh idea and a strong desire to successfully bring it to market would be wise in taking advantage of a 21st century approach to transforming creativity into dollars. It's about time for *Blue Sky Project Management*.

Chapter 1

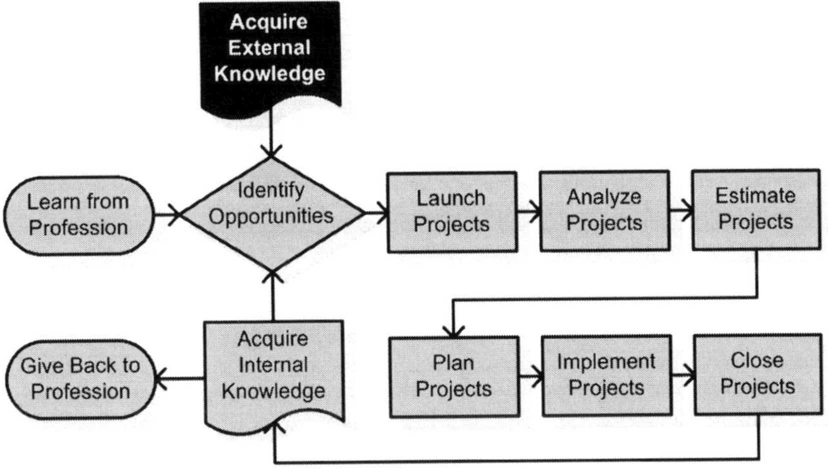

Keeping Pace with the Demand for Innovation

In the corporate world, innovation is currently at the top of the priority list for most executives focused on establishing or maintaining a strategic advantage. Major consulting firms regularly find that innovation is a key strategic focus for a majority of executives in the 21st century. Companies are busy investing in innovation projects to bolster their patent portfolios and reinforce barriers to entry in existing markets. However, most companies are still immature in their approach to managing innovation activities. This immaturity is exemplified in an overall low return on investment in their innovation pipelines. The biggest challenges facing most companies today are globalization, organizational issues, and leadership. Addressing these issues will help companies make the transition to leading their markets through innovation. It is clear that sharpening the ability to innovate is a necessary component to growth. The importance of innovation in the corporate world is shared by most executives, but just wanting to innovate does not mean much; it takes a systematic approach to be successful. Furthermore, the innovation alone is not necessarily going to provide a sustainable competitive advantage. It's the pace of innovation that serves as the secret ingredient. A systematic approach to bringing innovation to market quickly and consistently is the secret sauce to winning in the 21st century. Our challenge is to embrace the pace of innovation set by the new global economy and learn how to become the best at managing innovation projects - often the most difficult to characterize and understand.

Executives must be good at spotting winning innovation early and supporting them fully, while eliminating those with low probabilities for success. Many great innovations share five primary factors:

1. **Relative Advantage:** Increased value over a similar product or service is measured by the end consumer of the innovation (not the inventor) and is often based on perception, not necessarily demonstrated utility. There are many emotional factors at play

during the evaluation of the innovation that the inventor typically never anticipates and probably doesn't understand. These factors explain how scientifically viable innovations sometimes fail in a fickle market.

2. **Compatibility:** The effort to switch to the new innovation must be less than the relative advantage to make it worthwhile for the end consumer. Also, the way the innovation is consumed must be aligned with the habits and belief systems of the consumer. Imagine trying to sell RFID tags embedded under the skin to help locate missing children. No matter how innovative the product, the belief systems of certain religious groups will deter its adoption in this particular market segment.

3. **Complexity:** The best innovations are easy to understand and use. They are dummy proof in their design and elegant in their delivery. Apple Computer is a leader in this domain with their world-class industrial design capabilities, user interfaces, and extreme attention to detail. An example of a poorly designed innovation would be, for example, the first generation video cassette recorders. When initially introduced to the market, programming these units to record was near impossible for the average consumer. Contrast this with the simplicity of modern day TiVo, which is highly intuitive.

4. **Trialability:** Skeptical consumers need to experience the innovation before they will hand over hard earned money to purchase. The easier an innovator makes this possible, the greater the adoption rate will be of the innovation. Imagine buying a new car without being allowed to test drive it. Today, much of the trialability of new products are performed virtually. Take the Home Shopping Network, for example, they are not just telling you about their products, but actually demonstrating them in use.

5. **Observability:** The more an innovation can be seen in use in our daily lives, the more inclined we are to adopt it. This factor can be linked to the explosion of viral marketing campaigns, such as Advergaming and product placement in movies. When we can see influential people in our social networks utilizing the benefits of an innovation we are instantly sold.

In addition to developing innovations that will rapidly scale the adoption curve, companies must also structure themselves in such ways that they can fully support the launch of an innovation. Many innovations become hamstrung by the outdated business structures of their sponsoring organizations. The most innovative companies are designed to take advantage of three primary drivers: speed to market, customization, and viral marketing.

Speed to Market

Research indicates that the average time-to-market for new product development is roughly 13 months and trending downward. Most companies attribute about one third of their revenues to new products, a trend which is increasing rapidly. The data indicates that companies are bringing more new products to market in shorter time periods. The drivers of improved throughput and capacity can be attributed to streamlined business processes allowing poor ideas to fail fast and great ideas to be fully resourced. Traditional product development processes typically consist of functional hand-offs and inefficient serial steps. Over the last two decades, new approaches like phased-gate decision points and cross-functional teaming have improved upon the inefficiencies, but have not solved the issues inherent in innovation projects. New research indicates that concurrent cross-functional development combined with robust knowledge management infrastructures can eliminate inefficiencies even further by removing the need for scheduled check points (a phased-gate requirement) in favor of real-time collaboration, which can only be performed efficiently in a projectized organization. Winning companies should learn to fully embrace project management in order to bring new innovations to market faster. In our global economy, large companies are no longer out performing small businesses. In fact, research indicates that size is no longer a factor. Fast companies are now beating slow companies in the market by bringing innovation to the consumer ahead of their competitors, thereby capturing first mover advantage and price premiums. We need only look at beta products proliferating the Internet by such renowned companies as Google, Apple, Yahoo, Microsoft, and many others, to understand that the rules of bringing products to market have changed in the 21st century.

In 1999 EDS managed a wholly owned subsidiary called Unigraphics Solutions (UGS). UGS was responsible for developing industrial design and manufacturing software. Their development time was roughly 12 months, typical for the industry in that year. The development process consisted of alpha releases, beta releases, and a series of release candidates, just to produce a single compact disk that was dropped in the mail in time to meet the planned launch date. Following the press release, UGS continued development with several months of bug fixes, then mass shipment and distribution to existing customers. Finally, customer support was deployed to assist with the complex installation process. UGS could count on an additional 12 months before most major customers could fully implement the new code, resulting in 24 months from concept to full deployment.

Fast forward five years and contrast the development efficiency of UGS with an application service provider in Hollywood, California called Iventa. The developers of Iventa deployed new code in a matter of hours (not years) to customers such as Metallica, Pamela Anderson, and Kid Rock. In some cases, key clients could call in the morning with an enhancement request and then test the new feature that same afternoon! Innovations in the delivery model of software utilizing the Internet changed the rules of the game to the point where the fastest companies are truly out performing the biggest.

To further make the point that speed to market is now king, let's examine the semiconductor industry. This business is largely driven by the average selling prices (ASP) of chips sold under short-term contracts and in the spot-market as commodities. ASPs decline an average of 11% per quarter over a market window that can span as little as 12 months. Companies in this industry attempt to recoup billion dollar investments within a short period of time and hope to make a profit before the ASPs drop below the cost of production. In this highly competitive industry, a week delay in schedule can equate to millions of dollars in lost revenue! A slip in product development by a quarter, or more, can eliminate all hopes for profitability and in some cases drive companies into the red.

Customization

It's no secret that customers want products and services that exactly meet their needs, exactly when they want them met. The good news is that they will often pay a premium for this level of satisfaction. The bad news is that it's nearly impossible for a company to deliver that degree of customization at reasonable cost structures. What can be accomplished, however, is near-customization by creating corporate structures that are less functional and more projectized. Figure 1.1 depicts a spectrum of project management adoption. The left end captures traditional functional organizations, such as many manufacturing companies, while the right end captures projectized organizations, such as NASA, for example. The center area, known as the balanced matrix, is most prevalent in companies employing knowledge workers.

PROJECT ADOPTION SPECTRUM

FIGURE 1.1

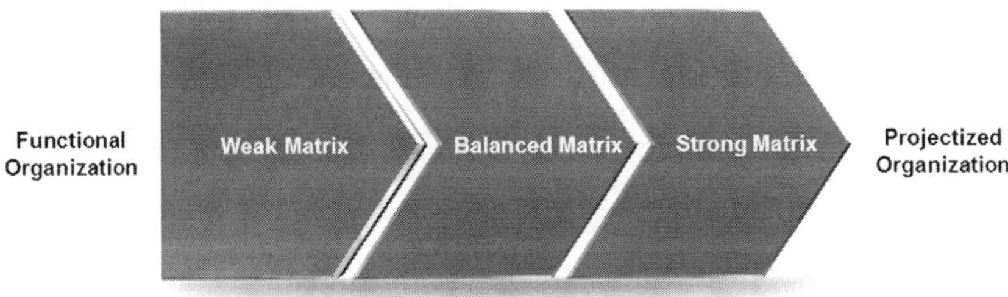

Projectized companies are organized to solve unique problems requiring unique results, while functional companies are designed to solve similar problems by applying routine operations and processes. Part of the challenge faced when embracing a culture of innovation is having the courage to transition organizational structures from functional silos to cross-functional teams, then ultimately to fully-functional project teams.

NASA is a good example of a projectized organization. They are organized around a portfolio of major programs run at each of nine Centers spread across the United States. In their storied culture, the program manager is king and calls the shots, while engineers are assigned to project teams based on their subject-matter expertise. As programs come to a close, project team members seek out new projects to join and contribute. This structure allows the President of the United States, for example, to request custom solutions, such as establishing human colonies on the moon, and NASA can respond.

Other industries requiring projectized structures are the movie industry and construction, to name a couple. Imagine for a moment what your particular industry or company would look like if it were structured around programs and projects. At the extreme end of this spectrum, there would be no need for an established corporate entity, or any functional groups for that matter. In fact, projects could be completed by assembling virtual teams of subject-matter experts located anywhere across the globe. Collaboration technology such as telepresence systems enable such a virtual structure to thrive today. It's not too difficult to imagine small groups of investors providing highly customized solutions to solve difficult problems by banding together virtual teams to implement a project, then disbanding them once the project is complete. Each member of the team contributes to the performance and the profitability of the project. Under this scenario, a team member's competence would dictate their demand in the global marketplace for talent. Virtual teaming is not mere speculation, this structure is currently operating globally in many industries. With our current level of technological advancement, the possibility of bringing together globally disbursed project teams for short-term engagements, then disbanding them after the project completes, is remarkable. Some executives are taking the concept of virtual teaming ever further by creating virtual companies. They are re-engineering their entire business structure to take advantage of the efficiencies offered by technology.

Viral Marketing

Have you ever heard of Advergaming? What about product placement? If not, you have certainly been exposed to the techniques. Think of the last movie you attended. Do you recall the various scenes showcasing a full line-up of a particular brand of vehicles? Chances are you left the movie with a clear impression of the types of vehicles available by a certain manufacturer. This is product placement at its best. Other examples include video gaming software developed around a particular product or service. Advergaming accomplishes what television and radio cannot, by reaching markets that are increasingly closed off from traditional media, both mentally and physically. Innovative companies with innovative products and services will do well to take advantage of these creative new channels for branding and awareness campaigns.

Other viral marketing channels include Internet sites that allow personal profiles to be saved and shared. These types of channels allow consumers of products and services to share their opinions (good and bad) in an informal and hopefully objective manner. It's in effect the reality TV of advertising and it works wonders. New products, services, and celebrities are born via video every day on the Internet. For example, *Journey*, the famous rock band, found their newest lead singer, Arnel Pineda, straight off of the Internet. More physical examples of viral marketing at work are the existence of product branded cars roaming the streets. Volkswagen accomplished buzz in the market when they offered the new Beetle free to influential members of society one year before they went on sale. Innovative companies must utilize new marketing channels to create a viral buzz among audiences that appreciate innovation. Nothing tops a personal endorsement from a trusted friend for a product or service. The challenge is to inspire the trusted friend enough so he or she becomes compelled to continuously make unsolicited endorsements to their networks.

Figure 1.2 plots speed to market, customization, and viral marketing according to their degree of adoption. The matrix identifies the types of new product development systems and business processes that are typically in use by companies according to their adoption.

MACULLEY MATRIX – *NEW PRODUCT DEVELOPMENT SYSTEMS*

FIGURE 1.2

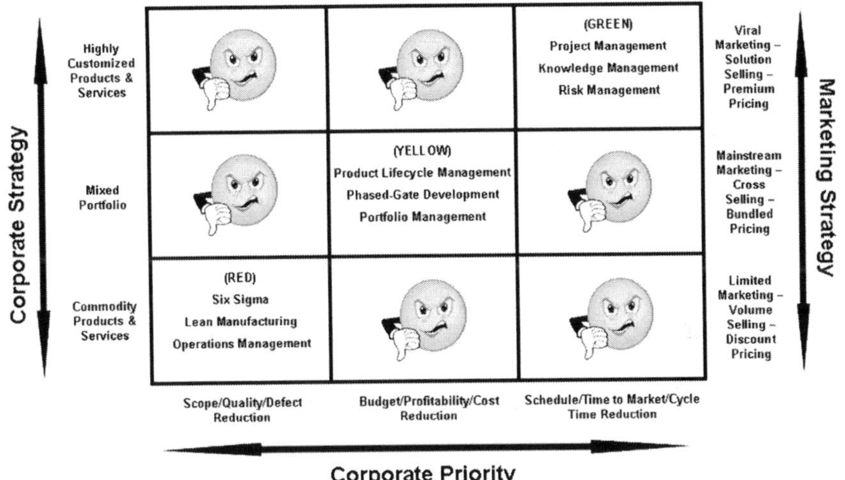

Innovation does not happen in a vacuum. Business processes are required to support the creative process and help guide that creativity toward a viable market solution as quickly as possible. Companies that have trouble innovating are often limited by their stale business processes, rather than a lack of good ideas. The paradox that executives face when making their companies more innovative is that more good management practice, in the traditional sense, will not allow them to reach their objective. Long-term business planning and more rigorous analysis of market conditions only causes businesses to fall into rat holes that divert their attention from what really matters. This paradox is even more pronounced when speaking of disruptive innovations. To be successful, we need to look beyond what worked in the past when tackling the challenges of the future. What worked fifty years ago is no longer effective.

20th Century Product and Service Development

There is an inherent conflict between traditional management practice and the development of modern day innovations. The factory-focused methodologies of the past are no longer effective. Traditional management methodology involves the idea of minimizing process variation by standardizing processes and taking control away from individuals, thereby creating the anti-innovation environment.

Six-Sigma

It can be argued that six-sigma is an overrated, albeit sacred cow, methodology for measuring and managing process variation. It certainly has its place in corporations with unchanging processes that handle high degrees of throughput. Pure manufacturing businesses, for example, could benefit from this systematic approach to defect reduction, however when viewed through the lens of innovation, it makes little sense. In innovative companies, engineering and manufacturing processes are changing constantly as new products come online. Product runs are also kept short to accommodate changing customer preferences and demand. Given these factors, six-sigma is simply ineffective in dynamic organizations. The opportunity to collect the amount of data required to produce meaningful statistics does not exist, and if it did, the process would be changed by the time the improvement was available. Research indicates that Asian countries are on the rise in their use of six-sigma as a business tool, while North America and Europe are on the decline. This trend maps with the migration of pure manufacturing work performed globally.

A lot of companies that have embraced six-sigma over the years (GE, Motorola) have learned the short comings first hand and have modified their approaches to the methodology, while still keeping the name for the sake of continuity. At the beginning of this century, in an attempt to drive six-sigma across its engineering organizations, GE had to modify their approach to the point where six-sigma more closely resembled traditional project management. At the time, GE called it six-sigma-light, but it was basically project management coupled with phased-gate decision points.

Lean Manufacturing

Lean manufacturing falls into the same category as six-sigma, in that it is only a viable business process when applied to pure manufacturing companies, with little place in the world of innovation. Management consultants tried to give six-sigma a facelift by calling it lean/six-sigma, but the end result was nothing more than business process re-engineering, or the more recent version known as business process optimization. Once again, this process is basically traditional project management with a different name.

Operations Management

Another 20th century concept is operations management. Still taught in most universities today, the subject has largely become stale and inapplicable to modern business. In a projectized organization, for example, the need for managing operations at an enterprise level is no longer required and may actually slow things down, assuming an enterprise even exists. Academics have caught on to this transition and are busy expanding and repackaging the subject under the banner of supply-chain management, which is much more applicable to 21st century companies. In some cases, networking, management information systems, and information technology are also falling under this new all inclusive banner.

Product Lifecycle Management

Product lifecycle management was the talk of the business community during the late 90s. It included a full-circle model for managing a product from concept to recycle, thereby opening up new markets for business system developers to enter. The idea was noble in that it had product responsibility pass from engineers to marketers, then to service providers and so on. The baton was handed to the next functional group as the product entered that phase of its lifecycle. Unfortunately the full model never took hold and for good reason. The overhead burden for implementing, staffing, and maintaining such a complex business system was more than the anticipated value of the solution and in some cases raised cost of goods sold for the client. Portions of the product lifecycle management model are still in place in many companies today, although they have morphed into more value added components. Many product lifecycle management software providers have given up on the model in favor of portfolio management.

Product Portfolio Management

There is a place for portfolio management in the 21st century, however the business process must manage projects instead of products. The assessment of a portfolio of products, as it is currently implemented, is somewhat narrow in focus given that most products are bundled with services, marketing, advertising, and many other components that enable them to come to market as a total solution. In a projectized company, the focus is on the viability of the entire project of which the product is only a part. True project portfolio management takes into consideration many factors, including the project's return on investment (ROI), strategic alignment, and market timing. Portfolio evaluations will be covered in greater detail in Chapter 2.

Phased-Gate Development

Much can be said for this product development business process, although it has shortcomings when applied to innovation management. The problems arise when projects with high degrees of uncertainty and short delivery times are applied. Under these scenarios, the decision point gates become somewhat arbitrary. When the gates are scheduled, they are often further out than the project requires, thereby allowing the work to fill the allotted time and slow time-to-market. The primary purpose of each gate in the phased-gate process is to reduce the financial risk to a company by giving managers the ability to kill a development before additional money is spent. In practice, however, much of the due diligence is performed upfront during the project launch phase. The project's value to the company is established and changes little during the development. The symptom of this reality is that most decision point meetings have transitioned from go/no go decision making to more like proceed with caution, or proceed full-steam ahead. In either case, the decision is to continue. Project management handles innovation more effectively than the phased-gate approach by including major milestones within the project's schedule. These are natural review points as the data is made available, rather than artificial gates with little correlation to the availability of relevant project information.

21st Century Product and Service Development

Risk Management

In traditional project management approaches, risk management is often an after thought. This may explain the unusually high project failure rate, especially among information technology projects.

Nevertheless, when dealing with innovation, where risk is exponentially higher than mere enhancement projects, the proper management of risk from the beginning to the end of the project is critical. The importance of risk management became real for me when the Space Shuttle *Columbia* exploded in 2003, while I was attending a NASA offsite strategy session in Boulder, Colorado. Surrounded by friends and colleagues of the astronauts on board during the explosion, the looks on their faces as they watched the disaster on a big screen television was indescribable. The truth of the matter is that all projects have risks, but innovation projects, in particular, are prone to failure due to poor risk management. Risk management is also used to help companies navigate new cultures and laws. For example, AgustaWestlandBell (AWB), the newly formed company that won the U.S. Presidential helicopter contract used enterprise risk management to minimize its political risk. Being primarily a British company and new to the complexities of U.S. government contracting, AWB was rightfully nervous about tripping up on unforeseen legal issues, that could cause a potential loss of the contract. Combine this with a gaggle of angry Senators, up in arms over the thought of a foreign company building our President's transportation and the risk environment was very high, as you can imagine. In this case, the most catastrophic outcome would have been a loss of contract, whereas in NASA's case it was measured as loss of life.

Not all projects have risks where the stakes are as high, but you can be sure that true innovation comes very close. Chapter 4 will cover risk management in more detail.

Knowledge Management

Knowledge management is one of the most exciting areas of focus in the business world today and quite possibly the most misunderstood. Executives have a hard time visualizing what this process could look like given the nature of the tools and methods in use. One such method that often takes people by surprise is storytelling. This simple practice, in place since the dawn of civilization, has proven to be quite effective, especially when sharing lessons-learned and best-practices. People love to hear about the highs and lows of a project directly from the leader. Through this process the information passes from those that have been there to those who will be soon. There is much more to knowledge management than just telling stories, of course. This important topic will be discussed further in Chapter 9. The interesting thing to consider is that knowledge management can be considered the new total quality management (TQM) made famous by Deming, Crosby, Juran, and others. It is how projectized organizations raise the bar from one project to the next, as a form of continuous improvement.

Project Management

Finally, we make it to the mother of all business processes, project management. This often underestimated approach to getting work done is just starting to get the recognition it deserves. One area where project management has filled a gap is in strategic planning. For years companies have been baffled as to why their brilliant strategies simply sit on a shelf collecting dust. The common scenario is as follows: executives spend weeks offsite thinking up mission statements and strategies only to return to the office and witness their employees continuing the status quo. Then twelve months later they are back offsite complaining about their incompetent workers and creating a new strategy. What's missing, of course, is a mechanism for linking strategy with operations.

Regarding innovation, project management is the way to add structure to what is a highly artistic endeavor. If you've ever experienced analysis paralysis or over engineering, then chances are the activity was not managed using *Blue Sky Project Management* techniques as described in this book. As the world changes, business and academic leaders alike must embrace new challenges by providing business processes that support and encourage innovation. Project management is the business process and, more precisely, *Blue Sky Project Management* is the methodology that will help innovators bring their ideas to market ahead of their competition.

The Challenge Ahead

Managing innovation requires an integration of risk management, knowledge management, and faster learning-cycles to be successful. This integration is enabled by fully-functional project teaming, real-time communication, and is led by project managers focused on maintaining a congruent project plan that exactly meets the needs of the end customer. Figure 1.3 depicts a flow where this integration is possible. The concept is simple enough, however it takes a highly skilled project manager to make music out of a team of subject-matter experts, each with their own unique instruments and attitudes.

MANAGING INNOVATION DIAGRAM
FIGURE 1.3

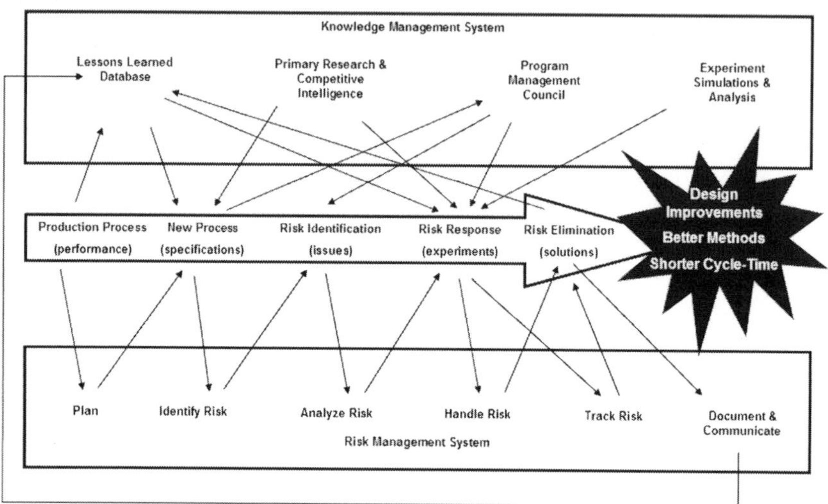

We are at the tipping-point of project management adoption on a global scale, across all industries, and in all countries. Combine this event with the evolution of the global economy from manufacturing and operations to innovation through collaborating across all functions and time zones, and you get exponential growth opportunities at our finger tips. The opportunities are emerging within a sea of cultural perspectives. Companies must learn to build generation-x businesses today and be poised to sell products and services to generation-y tomorrow. But like all changes involving cultural paradigm shifts, it's important not to under estimate the incumbents, also known as baby boomers. This shift will certainly not be easy to accomplish. Taking the lead in bringing about change is never an easy undertaking. The status quo is strongly defended by those with a vested interest in keeping things the way they are, while supporters of change are often hesitant to take a bold stand in the face of an uncertain future. The change-agent is often positioned in the middle of what seems like a sea of hostile ambivalence.

It's high-time for a revolution in how we get work done, how we link strategy to operations, and how we innovate beyond our wildest imaginations. In short, it's time for *Blue Sky Project Management*.

Chapter 2

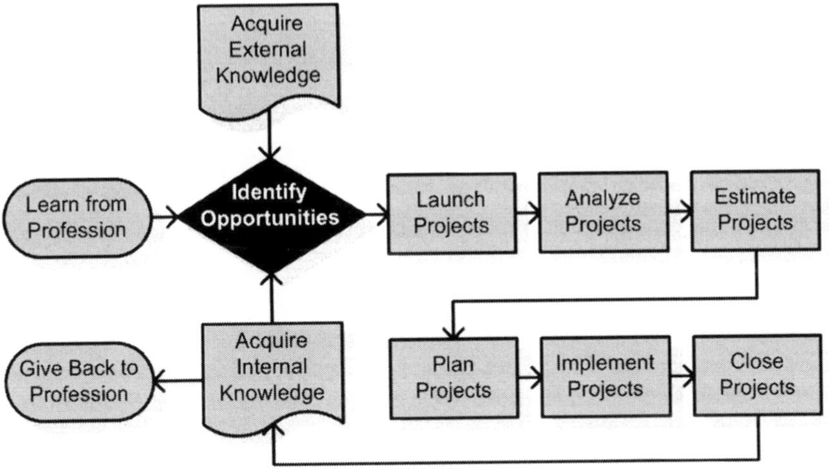

Identifying *Blue Sky* Opportunities

Where do project opportunities come from? Many companies operate from a tactical mindset, applying resources to their most pressing problems. Unfortunately, this leaves little time or energy to work on strategic initiatives, which are the activities on our agendas that are very important, but not necessarily urgent. This non-urgency is where the issue lies; we can put them off while we tackle the less important, but highly urgent matters, such as emails, phone calls, and the like. It's easy to get caught up in the immediate gratification of checking things off of our to-do list each day, while ignoring the most important and strategic items for another day. This is a shallow sense of accomplishment that typically ends in disaster as those important items, which never get attended to, eventually come to a head. We often know what we should be working on, but have a hard time visualizing the steps involved in linking strategy to operations. One such method of linking strategy to operations involves a visual representation of a company's strategy from a series of perspectives.

Strategic Visualization

What seems like a simple task of doing what needs to be done from a strategic point of view is much more difficult in practice. Most executives have a hard time operationalizing their visions. Although strategy has never been more important to executives, research indicates that companies consistently fail to execute successfully. Using outdated management practices is the primary cause. In the 21st century, executives must learn to translate their visions into activities across their enterprises.

To address this challenge, strategic visualization techniques have been developed. This technique begins with a company's vision/mission statement, then is followed by a series of perspectives by which the vision/mission statements can be perceived. Typically the perspectives are in order with financial at the top, followed by customer, internal, and enablers at the bottom of the matrix. However, the types of perspectives and order can be customized for the company. Each perspective is then populated with a group of objectives, such as growing revenue and improving productivity for the financial perspective, for example. Customer perspective objectives may be improving brand image, increasing product availability, and creating a purchase experience. Internal perspective objectives could be to improve operations, manufacturing capacity, or cross-functional communications. Enablers are often system related, such as developing a knowledge management infrastructure. Each of these high-level objectives should then be fleshed out to include a measurement metric, target outcome, and ultimately an initiative. These initiatives then become the portfolio of strategic opportunities. Notice they are not yet strategic projects, since the opportunities have yet to be chartered as official projects. In summary, the strategic visualization technique prescribes the following sequence:

Vision and Strategy → Perspectives → Objectives → Measures → Targets → Initiatives

When deploying strategic visualization in an organization, as depicted in Figure 2.1, especially one that is functionally structured, it is common to have one corporate chart with subordinate charts for each functional department. Once the initiatives have been converted into chartered projects, it is helpful to view these in the form of a roadmap.

STRATEGIC VISUALIZATION DIAGRAM
FIGURE 2.1

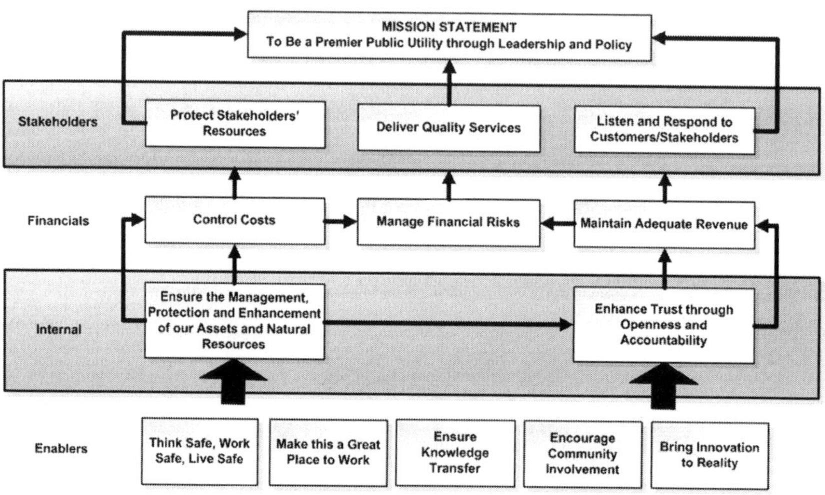

Road Mapping

Also known as sausage charts, roadmaps can be a great way of visualizing the timing of a series of strategic projects. This is helpful in large organizations where there may be hundreds of projects in play at any given point in time. Roadmaps can be as simple as a horizontal line starting at the inception of a project and ending at the completion, as depicted in Figure 2.2.

ROADMAP DIAGRAM

FIGURE 2.2

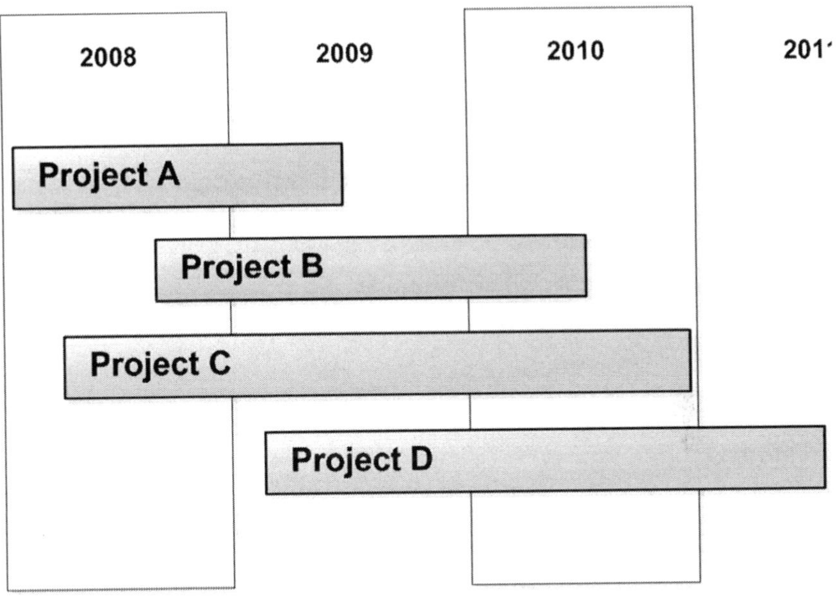

Organizations utilizing phased-gate development may also segment the line according to their defined stages of product development. From this high-level visual, executives can derive the percent complete of various initiatives, as well as the overall resource burden on the organization. Roadmaps can be used for projects, products, or even pure technology development initiatives. There are numerous reasons why road mapping is important, such as:

- Road mapping aids in the planning process by capturing cross-functional initiatives.

- Roadmaps allow companies to view initiatives in relation to time, thereby enabling high-level portfolio analysis.
- Roadmaps force project teams to address the beginning and end dates of an initiative.
- Roadmaps reveal gaps in technology plans and resource requirements.
- Roadmaps enable tradeoff analysis by forcing initiatives to be depicted in a common format.
- Road mapping helps set more competitive and realistic targets by enabling comparisons with industry and competitor plans.
- Roadmaps provide a guide to cross-functional teams and helps keep staff on the same page.
- Sharing roadmaps allows departments to understand all the initiatives planned across an enterprise and highlights opportunities for consolidation and leverage.
- Road mapping facilitates communication with customers, partners, and external vendors.
- Road mapping builds a common vocabulary and aids in the communication process among newly formed teams.

Another great visual technique for linking strategy with operations involves the development of a strategic profile for initiatives.

Strategic Profile

When seeking to identify break-through opportunities that create new market demand and disrupt competitive landscapes, the use of strategic profiling can provide tremendous insight into many potential opportunities. This process begins with the identification of key factors representing an existing initiative, such as price, convenience, functionality, and so forth. Once these factors are identified and validated, then existing substitutes to this initiative are mapped according to their degree (high/low) of achieving the given factors, as depicted in Figure 2.3.

STRAGIC PROFILE DIAGRAM
FIGURE 2.3

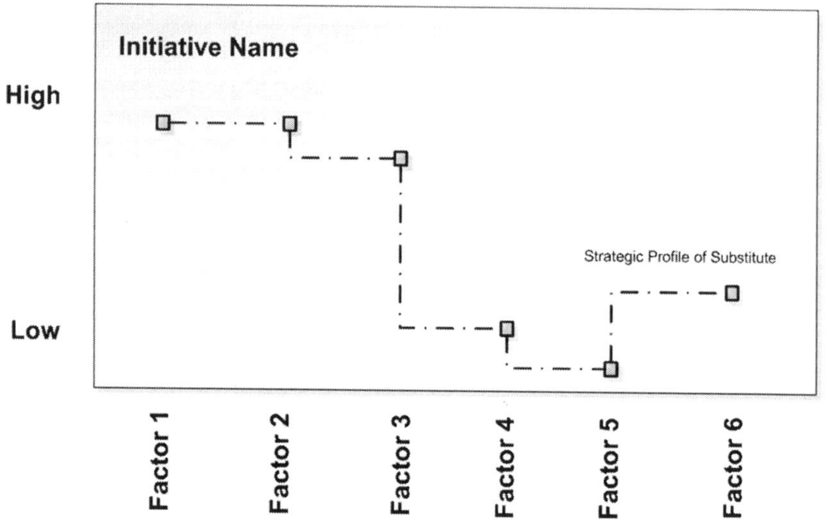

What results is a strategic profile curve (line graph) that depicts that particular substitute's value proposition to the company or market. Substitutes are not specific companies, but rather solutions to a problem statement. Once all the available solutions are mapped for a given problem, it can become obvious where unmet value lies, or new factors are missing. To create a new strategic profile, the project team should look for gaps. Factors of substitute solutions that are not critical to solving the problem statement should be eliminated. Factors that are not primary drivers to solving a problem, yet add secondary value should be reduced in their overall contribution to the solution, while the primary drivers are increased. The most important step is the identification of new factors that current solutions do not contain, yet are key to solving the problem statement in a unique and compelling way.

Strategic Opportunity Portfolios

Once a set of initiatives or opportunities have been assembled, then each one must be organized into opportunity themes for further analysis. The portfolio should be considered as a group of market opportunities, rather than pre-solved projects. It is common for executives to want to jump to the solution at this point, without fully understanding all aspects of the opportunity at hand, however a little patience at this stage will pay dividends in the future. The benefits of a portfolio approach to opportunity evaluation are too numerous to list, however a few of the more common are as follows:

- Builds discipline into project selection process
- Links project selection to strategic metrics
- Prioritizes project proposals across a common set of criteria, rather than on politics or emotion
- Allocates resources to projects that align with strategic direction

- Balances risk across all projects
- Justifies killing projects that do not support organizational strategy
- Improves communication and supports agreement on project goals

Opportunity Themes

Opportunity themes are simply high-level problem statements that encompass a family of related issues. Typically, the biggest problem with a poorly structured opportunity theme is that the themes combine multiple opportunities into a single statement. It is critical that the opportunity themes address a single thought and contain enough information that a potential solution path can be derived. For example a poor opportunity theme may read as follows;

Military fighter jets have reached a plateau in performance capability and cost efficiency as measured in operating hours between major service intervals because of higher than ideal weight to thrust requirements, inefficient operating capabilities above 50,000 Ft., component material properties existing at the edge of their temperature envelope, and lack of part standardization across military platforms.

Its important to note that this opportunity lies in the fact that the entire aerospace industry is experiencing the plateau. Therefore, the first company to overcome the barriers to rising above the plateau wins market share. This problem statement has many issues. First of all, it combines more than a single major opportunity to be evaluated. Secondly, it is too vague to be measured effectively, and finally, it assumes the cause in the statement, which has the effect of prescribing the solution. In many cases the cause is known, however it should be left out of the opportunity theme unless it is certain to relate to the effect. Perhaps a better version can be broken into several high-level themes that read as follows:

Example Opportunity Themes (High-Level Problem Statements)

1. *Aircraft thrust to weight ratio more than 50:1*
2. *High altitude turbine thrust capability above 50,000 Ft*
3. *Turbine engine performance improvement beyond 1,200 F*
4. *Parts standardization cost reduction greater than 15% of all DoD aircraft*

As you can imagine, each of the revised statements will require a unique solution, therefore a unique opportunity plan would be required to evaluate further. If a project team were to take on the original problem statement, they would have a hard time characterizing the issues and understanding how project success would be measured in the mind of the sponsors. Also, the scope would be so large that the duration and cost of the project would exceed what is considered prudent. Being crystal clear upfront when defining the opportunity can eliminate a lot of heartache and miscommunication downstream. Once the opportunities are clearly understood and documented, they can be converted into opportunity plans.

Opportunity Plans

From clear opportunity themes, opportunity plans can be derived. But what makes them different than project plans? Opportunity plans are only prepared for the purpose of evaluation and approval to convert a opportunity theme into a project. Only a minimal amount of information is required to proceed to the evaluation stage. Obviously, it makes little sense to spend an in exorbitant amount of time developing fully defined project plans for opportunities that may not get approved and funded. It's best to keep them short and to the point in preparation for the evaluation stage. According to the *Blue Sky* method of project management, only the following items are necessary to proceed to the evaluation stage:

1. *Opportunity theme and description*
2. *Potential project approach*
3. *Rough order of magnitude project duration estimate (-25%/+75% of nominal)*
4. *Rough order of magnitude project cost estimate (-25%/+75% of nominal)*

Using the *Blue Sky* approach and one of the revised opportunity themes presented earlier in this Chapter, we can create the following opportunity plan:

Opportunity Theme

Turbine engine performance improvement beyond 1,200 F

Opportunity Description

An opportunity exists in the military aerospace market for companies that can produce a turbine jet engine that can operate with hot gas path temperatures in the range of 1,200-1,800 degrees

F. By operating at higher temperatures, customers will be able to increase the thrust of existing aircraft without major structural modifications. The opportunity solution will also enable customers to upgrade aircraft performance by utilizing retrofitted jet engines instead of engaging in new aircraft development. The potential cost savings for the customer is estimated to be $10 billion.

Potential Project Approach

There are several approaches that can be pursued when increasing the temperature capability of the hot gas path section of the turbine engine. Improved cooling schemes and the use of ceramic materials as a replacement for nickel based alloys are two of the most promising developments that can be leveraged in this project. The primary failure points when operating above 1,200 F are known to be the turbine airfoils and the combustion heat shield, therefore it is recommended that the scope of this project include the development and successful testing within the specified operating envelope of these two components using a combination of material changes and cooling schemes. Other approaches will also be investigated as they relate to these two primary paths.

ROM Project Duration Estimate

17.3 months [Te = (O+M4+P)/6]

Optimistic = 12 months; Most Likely = 16 months; Pessimistic = 28 months

ROM Project Cost Estimate

$758,333 [Te = (O+M4+P)/6]

Optimistic = $525,000; Most Likely = $700,000; Pessimistic = $1,225,000

Most schedule and cost estimates at this point in the process are back of the envelope analysis based on historical data. During the opportunity evaluation and selection stage, the project sponsor should be prepared to sign up for the pessimistic estimates for duration and cost, as worst case scenario.

Opportunity Evaluation and Selection

The best opportunity evaluation methodologies are void of politics, emotion, and have achieved buy-in from the decision makers who will use it. To accomplish this, it is important to plan on several iterations in a working group to debate and agree on critical objectives, their weightings, and their respective metrics. The purpose of this exercise is to produce a corporate opportunity evaluation matrix by which all opportunities will be assessed. An evaluation matrix allows stakeholders to consistently assess projects using established criteria that support the strategic goals and objectives of their companies. Using this approach, executives can identify those initiatives that are "must haves" and make tradeoff decisions with less strategic options.

Evaluation Matrix

Spreadsheets work best when developing your custom evaluation matrix. The structure is quite simple, however agreement on the content is somewhat challenging. Along the left hand column you will want to list your company's top five objectives in order of importance, with the most important at the top. Objectives may include high-level goals, reduce product development time, increase learning rate, and the like. It is also important to include an objective associated with strategic alignment, although this one is often of lower importance. Once your list of objectives is complete, each one should be weighted on a scale of 1-5. A weight of 5 means the objective is of the utmost importance, while a 1 means it is somewhat important. Note that all objectives in your matrix should be considered important. Feel free to experiment with larger weighting ranges to capture the magnitude of importance between each objective in a more granular way. Along the top row will be a variation of a Likert scale as follows:

1. Opportunity cannot be measured
2. Expect minimal improvement from opportunity
3. Expect moderate improvement from opportunity
4. Expect high improvement from opportunity
5. Expect significant improvement from opportunity

The top row is also weighted, allowing a multiplier with the objectives along the left column, thereby enabling an opportunity to be assigned a score. Included within the body of the matrix should be ranges of metrics that apply to the corresponding objectives on the left and scale along the top row. Figure 2.4 depicts and example of an opportunity matrix.

OPPORTUNITY MATRIX

FIGURE 2.4

Project Name:		New Product X					
Project Description:							
		Improvement Cannot be Measured	Expect Minimal Improvement	Expect Moderate Improvement	Expect High Improvement	Expect Significant Improvement	
		0	-1	-2	-3	-4	Score
Manufacturing Cycle Time Reduction	-4	-	(< 2% MCT)	(> = 2% MCT)	(> = 5% MCT)	(> = 10% MCT)	8
		0	0	1	0	0	
Number of Learning Cycle Reduction	-3	-	(< 5% LCT)	(> = 5% LCT)	(> = 10% LCT)	(> = 20% LCT)	9
		0	0	0	1	0	
Cost Reduction/ Cost Avoidance	-2	-	(< $500K Savings within 12 Months)	(> = $500K Savings within 12 Months)	(> = $1M Savings within 12 Months)	(> = $5M Savings within 12 Months)	2
		0	1	0	0	0	
Strategy Map Alignment	-1	Does Not Support Strategy Map	Directly Contributes to Strategic Enabler Indicator	Directly Contributes to Strategic Enabler and Internal Indicator	Directly Contributes to Strategic Enabler, Internal, and Customer Indicator	Directly Contributes to Strategic Enabler, Internal, Customer, and Financial Indicator	4
		0	0	0	0	1	
TOTAL		Tier 2 - High Priorty					23

Notice that ROI is not included as an objective in the matrix since innovation projects often have unknown returns. Experience has shown that when ROI is required on opportunities with high uncertainty, such as innovation projects, the estimates are more wild guesses than anything else.

Choosing Your Best Opportunity

People love to argue in the grey areas, so avoid this outcome by ensuring your evaluation matrix and preliminary scope statements are as clear and objectively written as possible. Also, be prepared to modify your evaluation matrix when the criteria and/or weightings do not makes sense. These tools are designed to be calibrated with use and modified as new data dictates. Ultimately, the best projects, whether selected using an evaluation matrix or not, are those that move your organization to a new level of performance, or satisfy a unique and challenging problem in the marketplace. Research indicates that project failure rates range between 55% and 75%, in that they don't meet their intended schedule, scope, and/or budget requirements. The exact number varies across project types and industries, with IT projects failing the most. Project failure is normally attributed to poor communication and planning, however experience indicates that this is only part of the answer. One big factor that rarely shows up on surveys is project team attitude. When project team members are excited about a project and feel it's important to their company, or society at large, then their performance naturally increases. The same is true in the opposite direction, when the perception is that the project is just busy work, or has a poorly defined problem statement. The excitement, relevance, and importance factors should all weigh into your overall project selection process to improve your success rates. A project team that is emotionally and mentally committed to the success of a project is the best recipe for achieving world-class results.

Chapter 3

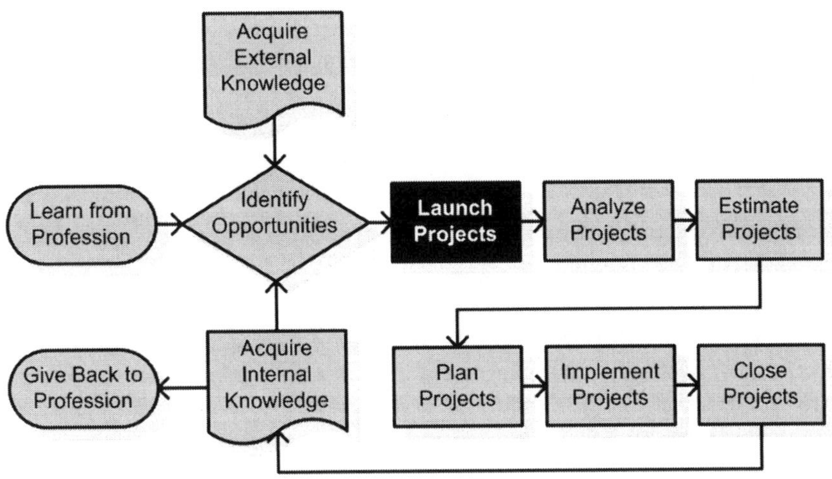

Launching a *Blue Sky* Project

In Chapter 2 we reviewed conceptually what makes a great opportunity plan, however in practice most innovation related problems have multiple nested issues. Projects can evolve from less precise plans, however it's better to deconstruct the opportunity into the main issues if at all possible. Let's assume opportunity theme number 2 from Chapter 2 was selected for a project. We can start with that language and define the problem we need to solve with our project. For example, when innovative companies engage in research, they may have a general problem statement such as:

Current turbine engine designs have achieved maximum performance efficiency due to hot gas path temperatures reaching the limits of nickel alloy material properties.

Once this general problem statement is identified, it's important that the project sponsor subdivide it into more specific problem statements, or experiments, that can eventually form sub-projects. Note that this fine-tuning should happen before the project manager is brought into the picture. This is a sponsor's responsibility. The result will be a group of related sub-problems organized under a common theme, or program. In the case of the problem statement above, we can develop the following program with sub-problem statements:

Program Theme: *Turbine Engine Performance Improvement*

Sub-Problem A: *Nickel alloy cannot exceed 1,200 degrees F without significant degradation of material properties*

Sub-Problem B: *Component surfaces in the hot gas path section of the turbine engine experience the highest temperatures, thereby causing cracking and disintegration*

These sub-problem statements may produce more than a single supporting project per problem. In fact, when innovating, it is desirable to implement as many projects, or experimental hypothesis, that a company can afford. When conducting research, for example, the solution path is not typically known, therefore multiple approaches should be investigated in parallel, when possible.

The Project Charter

Once opportunities are identified, evaluated, and selected, then problem statements can be properly defined, which means they sufficiently capture the issues associated with the program themes. Finally, these problem statements are ready to become official *Blue Sky* projects. The first step in initiating a project is to charter it. Chartering a project makes it official and links it to the ongoing work of the organization. According to traditional project management methodologies, the primary content of the project charter should be a concise problem statement and its relative importance to the organization, the purpose of the project in solving the problem, a brief understanding of customer requirements, and a description of the intended product, service, or result. Also required are the names of the project's sponsor and assigned project manager, as well as the project manager's authority level. Finally, any known milestone dates, assumptions, and constraints, such as financial and resource, should be listed.

In reality, most companies skip the project chartering step completely, since they are eager to get to work and fail to see the value in the charter activity. Combine this apprehension with the fact that innovation projects have high degrees of uncertainty and unknown requirements, and you can imagine why charters get ignored. The low rate of project chartering can also be attributed to the fact that project sponsors are the intended authors of charter documentation. These executives typically do not have a strong understanding of project management practices, nor the time to spend in completing the document. However, an argument can be made for completing a much reduced version of the project charter. There are really only three things that are important to capture at this stage of the process:

1. A clearly defined problem statement
2. The name and title of the project sponsor
3. The name of the assigned project manager

Including information beyond the three items listed above begins to overlap with the development of the project scope, schedule, and budget documentation that will begin following an approved charter document. The desires of both the project sponsor and the assigned project manager are fairly clear with regard to the charter. The sponsor is driven to ensure the problem that needs to be solved is clearly documented and that there is a resource assigned with the task of finding a solution. The project manager is driven to ensure the project has a clearly identified sponsor who will support and fund the project, as well as ensure that he or she has been officially granted the authority to manage.

The Preliminary Scope Document

The preliminary scope document should contain just enough information to allow a project team to develop a preliminary schedule and budget, but not more. It's common for the scope document to be reduced in requirements once the sponsor understands the necessary cost and time duration to deliver the initially conceived project deliverables. Therefore it makes more sense for a project team to begin the iterative process of achieving congruency between the triple-constraints of scope, schedule, and budget, rather than spending too much time trying to get the scope document perfect before developing the schedule and budget. The opportunity plan developed during the evaluation stage can be utilized in the development of the preliminary scope document. Also, many of the items previously identified as charter requirements now make sense to include in the preliminary scope document. Traditional project management methodologies describe the preliminary scope document as outlining what needs to be accomplished, including project objectives. This includes the boundaries of the project, or what will be included and what will not, project deliverables, and their respective acceptance criteria. The characteristics, requirements, and functionality of the project's intended product, service, or results should be documented. Also included should be the project's organization, risks, schedule milestones, work breakdown structure, and cost estimate.

Once again, the recommended activity of the traditional approach to project management seems to overlap with other steps in the process, such as development of the schedule, budget, and risk register, in this case. As traditional project management methodologies define the charter and scope documents, they are redundant with one another. The primary purpose of the preliminary scope documents, as stated previously, is to provide enough definition of the project to allow the creation of a preliminary schedule and budget. To accomplish this outcome, the following items are recommended:

1. Project title, purpose, and description
2. Project objectives
3. Project deliverables
4. Project boundaries, assumptions, and constraints

High-Temp Turbine Project

Purpose and Description

The ideal language for this section of the preliminary scope document should provide the reader with a comprehensive visual representation of the reason for pursuing the project, as well as its intended approach and flow. To accomplish this, it is recommended that the project get mapped back to the problem statement, the approved opportunity, the corporate strategic objective, and ultimately the corporate vision. In terms of the description of the project, text is often sufficient, however including a mock-up of the expected product, service, or result is very effective when this information is available. When developing software applications, for example, the user interface is often difficult to describe with words. A visual depiction of the user interface can eliminate a lot of time consuming and costly modifications downstream. Using Sub-Problem A from earlier in this Chapter, we can develop the following project purpose and description:

To achieve our vision of leading the global advancement of military aerospace performance, we have established a three year corporate objective of improving turbine engine performance by 20%. One of the primary factors currently affecting performance involves the degradation of nickel alloy material properties when operating above 1,200 degrees F. To overcome this issue, a project has been approved to investigate and develop a marketable solution. The project team will investigate commercially available materials that maintain their properties at temperatures between 1,200-1,800 F, as well as materials in development, but not yet commercially available. Some initial candidate materials that will be investigated are powdered metals, ceramics, and carbon matrix composites. All hot gas path engine components will be researched as candidates for material substitution, however emphasis will be placed on the high-pressure turbine airfoils, combustion chambers, and heat shields.

Project Objectives

1. *Further our understanding of high-temp material property degradation between 1,200-1,800 degrees F*
2. *Further our understanding of thermal dynamics principles between 1,200-1,800 F*
3. *Further our understanding of manufacturing capabilities of high-temp materials*
4. *Further our understanding of the incremental performance improvements gained by increased combustion temperature*

Project deliverables

1. *Research report characterizing candidate material that maintain their properties up to 1,800 degrees F*
2. *Research report characterizing the current temperature profiles and ranges of all candidate hot gas path components*
3. *Working prototype of selected hot gas path component designed using selected high-temp material*
4. *Research report recommending modified turbine engine design capable of sustaining operating temperatures between 1,200-1,800 degrees F based off of analysis from working prototype*

Project boundaries, assumptions, and constraints

The project team will perform its research using the JTAGGIII engine prototype as the baseline configuration. Component manufacturing will be either performed by GE or outsourced to specialty vendors as required. All assembly and testing will be performed in GE facilities. It is understood that this project will operate under U.S. secret security clearance regulations and that all staff members working on this project must have a valid U.S. secret security clearance and be a U.S. citizen in good standing. All vendors working on this project will be verified as approved to work on U.S. secret security contracts. All GE facilities where assembly and testing occurs will be compliant with U.S. secret security regulation. It is assumed that the funding for this project will be made available in one lump sum at the beginning of the project and that a JTAGGIII engine prototype will be made available for modification. All research reports will be delivered in Adobe PDF format with an accompanying compact disk. Pressures and temperatures will be measured at sea level. Stress analysis and heat transfer models will be produced using Ansys software.

Sponsor Review of Preliminary Scope Document

When your preliminary scope document is complete, it's important to prepare for a face-to-face meeting with the project sponsor to review the project and gain buy-in. The ideal communication during this meeting helps the stakeholder visualize the stages of the project and the end result. One of the best ways to accomplish this task is to develop a story-board, similar to what would be created during the development of a television commercial. Sketch out your story-board with paper and pencil, trying to capture the main message, or point of each stage of the project. The ideal number of scenes in your story-board is five to ten, depending on the complexity of the project. Once the story-board is complete, draw squares around each of the scenes; these will represent individual Power Point slides. The purpose of story-boarding is to help organize the flow and pace of the message. For example, assume we are building a story-board for the High-Temp Turbine Project. The first scene may depict a series of material types, a material science laboratory, a heat transfer diagram, special tooling required for manufacturing processes, such as atomic deposition. The collage of images should capture the main point of this stage in the project, which is that research will be conducted on high-temp materials. Edit the collage as necessary to ensure it depicts the intent of the activities. From this pencil and paper collage, you can begin to create your Power Point slide capturing the message.

Start by inserting actual pictures of images on the blank Power Point slide in place of the images you drew on the respective paper drawing. For example, a rectangle box with the words "atomic deposition tool" can be replaced with an image of the actual tool downloaded from the vendors website. Where you captured material types with circles and the name of the material, insert a table listing out some of the material properties. You get the idea. Once you have all of your hand sketched images captured on your Power Point slide, begin to add text where clarification is necessary. The trick is to produce a slide that conveys the message with as few words as possible. Colors, symbols, charts, graphs, and pictures should make up 80% or more of the slide where possible. Simply slamming out a boring list of bullet-points will not evoke the emotion that is required to truly engage the sponsor in the project. Your goal is to help the sponsor see the end from the beginning as close to the way you see it as possible. By sharing the vision together, you, as the project manager, will experience more support and less confusion throughout the course of the project. A little extra effort upfront will pay dividends into the future.

Walking into a meeting armed with a world-class presentation is a great confidence booster, but don't make the mistake of focusing the meeting on the Power Point slides. The purpose of the presentation should be to provide background information and help solidify points made during a conversation, but not replace a conversation. The project sponsor is not only judging the merits of your proposed project, but also your confidence in your ability to lead the project and your capability to persuade and inspire. Project team members want to follow project leaders, not merely project administrators, so be sure to demonstrate to the sponsor that the project and the team are in good hands.

Other tactics that ensure a successful meeting are the use of physical props. In the case of the example project, it would be interesting to bring various material samples, or even a metallic airfoil to the meeting. By holding the props, the sponsor is able to learn about the project in a tactile way. This reinforces the visual slide presentation and the auditory conversation. Scents can also be incorporated into these types of meeting when applicable to the project. The idea is to approach the meeting with the sponsor in a sophisticated manner, taking into consideration the way humans convert information into understanding, then ultimately into emotion. A perfect example of someone who has perfected this type of exchange is Steve Jobs, CEO of Apple Computer. By the time Steve completes one of his annual Macworld events his audience is eating out of his hands. Some have likened Steve's presentations as a spiritual adventure; inspiring, imaginative, and innovative, just like the products he is selling. When watching Steve in action there are five main ingredients that rise to the surface:

1. Selling the audience on the value
2. Orchestrated delivery and mastery of the content
3. Using graphics and video to make key points
4. Conveying passion for the technology and the opportunity
5. Closing the presentation with an additional gold nugget

Finally, it's important to understand the "WIFM" of the project sponsor. This is the *What's In it For Me* component of the conversation that should not go unaddressed. Do not underestimate the importance of not only identifying the WIFM, but also ensuring the project fulfills it. Unfortunately, the discovery process is no simple feat. Most project sponsors will never reveal their true purpose for endorsing a particular project. Often these drivers are tied to ego, such as the need to feel important, or intelligent, or innovative. These are the primary characteristics of human behavior and play a huge factor in how strongly a project will be supported. For example, if you can gather that the hypothetical project sponsor of our high-temp turbine project has a need to be perceived as innovative within his professional circle, then it would be wise to point out the innovative aspects of the project, supported by a few fact-based sound bites that the sponsor can use after the meeting to justify his endorsement of the project to his peers. Anticipating the personal needs of the sponsor and equipping them with data that can help move their image in the organization, as well as their career, forward, is a winning proposition and one that will be rewarded with enthusiasm and funding.

Paying attention to the soft-skills of project management requires an appreciation for sophisticated techniques in communication, cognitive psychology, and neuro linguistic programming. Acumen in these areas differentiates average project managers from world-class leaders of innovation projects.

Chapter 4

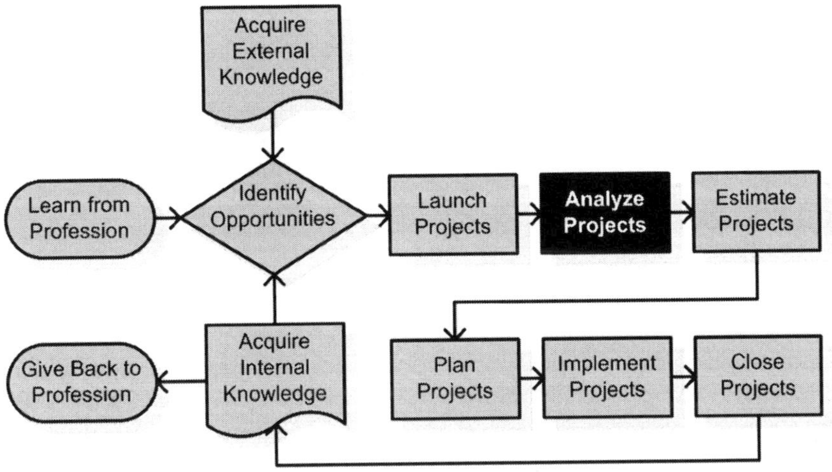

Analyzing Stakeholders and Risks

Innovation projects require a thorough analysis of the people involved with the funding, design, implementation, as well as the end-use of the product, service, or result. Anyone that can affect a project, or might be affected by its outcome is considered a stakeholder. Stakeholders can be people, groups, or organizations that have an interest in or may be affected, either positively or negatively, by a project's product, service, or result. Once you begin to think of all the people that can fit the broad definition of a stakeholder, the list can become very lengthy. It's helpful to organize the list into categories that further define the type of stakeholder in question.

One of the most effective methods involves the grouping of stakeholders by their degree of control over the project. When applying this concept to project management and the categorization of stakeholders, it's helpful to capture the entire universe using three levels of control with everyone else falling into the area of non-concern. Figure 4.1 depicts the relationship of the three circles.

CIRCLE OF CONTROL DIAGRAM
FIGURE 4.1

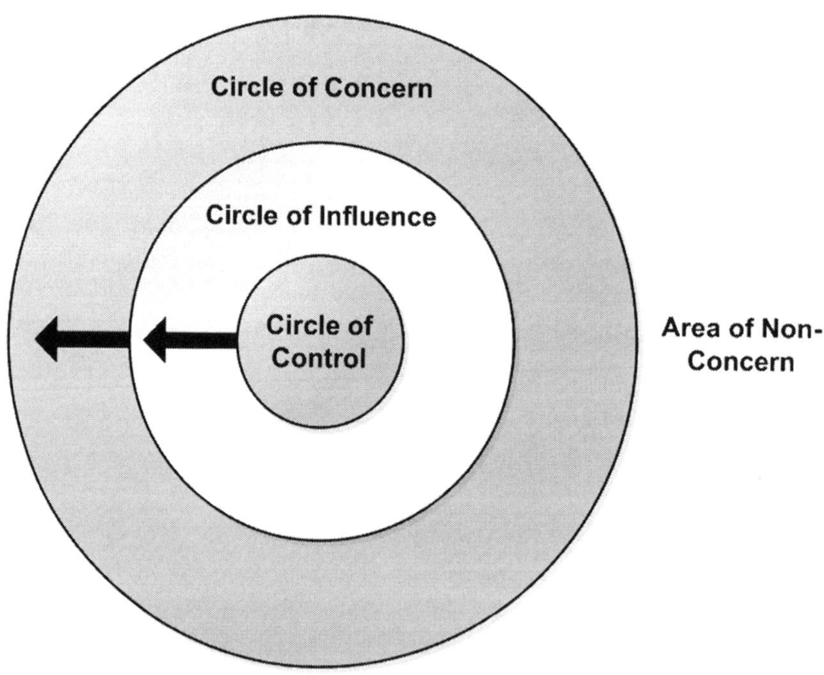

Circle of Control

This category of stakeholders can be defined as having the direct ability to cancel a project. Typically this circle would include the project's sponsor, primary customers, company executives, as well as a project's steering committee, if one exists. When listing out this category, specificity is critical. Members of this circle should be listed by name and title. For example, using the words "corporate executives" as a catch all is not sufficient. It is recommended that each member of the executive team who has the ability to cancel a project be specifically named, like John Smith, VP of Engineering. Personally naming individuals pays off when attempting to mitigate the risk of project cancellation. This category should be limited in number, with most large projects having fewer than a dozen stakeholders listed.

Circle of Influence

This category of stakeholders is larger in number than the control group. Typical inductees include project team members, vendors and suppliers of various deliverables, as well as department managers providing project resources. Less specificity is required when listing out members of this category. For example, listing "project team members" is appropriate. The need to list specific names and titles is not necessary. Influence can be thought of as the ability to either positively or negatively affect a project's outcome. A project team member that is confused about the objectives of the project could influence a project by that person making incorrect decisions. Another example could be a department manager who is not clear on the importance of a project to the corporation. This person could limit available resources, thereby jeopardizing the project.

Circle of Concern

The largest of the three circles, this category of stakeholders includes large organizations, external policy makers, coalitions, and some end users. For example, a project to develop a new fighter jet would be of concern to USAF fighter pilots. Individually this group represents thousands of people, but collectively their concerns can be addressed by the project manager. This category should be vague in their description of the members due to the shear size of the groups. In some instances, large groups can exert some influence on a project, in which case they should be moved into the circle of influence. At the beginning of a project, the exact classification of many stakeholders is unknown, so moving them around as more information is gained should be expected. The best project managers proactively manage all of the stakeholders through effective communication.

Once all of your project stakeholders have been identified and categorized, the next step is to evaluate them according to two primary criteria: their degree of interest in the project (along the Y axis) and their power to affect a project either negatively or positively (along the X axis). Using a 2x2 matrix as depicted in Figure 4.2 helps visualize the dispersion of stakeholders. The result will be four macro-level groups: high/high, high/low, low/high, and low/low.

HIGH/LOW DIAGRAM
FIGURE 4.2

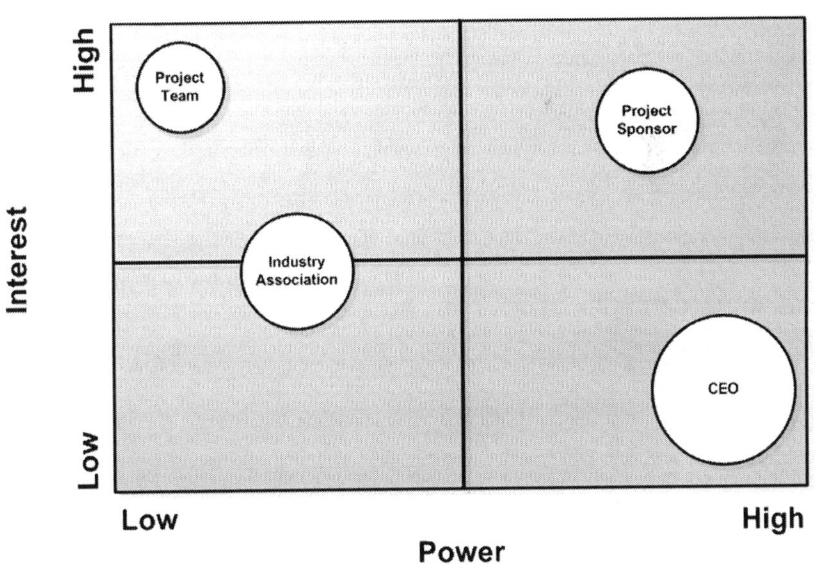

High/High (Interest/Power)

This group deserves special attention when it comes to communicating. Most stakeholders in the circle of control will fall into this quadrant. The most effective way to ensure clear communication is in face-to-face discussions, when possible. Typically, communications need to be frequent and concise. A one-on-one discussion of the top project risks and issues supported by a well designed executive dashboard is ideal. It's important to scrutinize the stakeholders that make it into the High/High group due to the level of overhead required to keep this group informed.

High/Low (Interest/Power)

This group typically wants to know the status of a project and be kept informed of issues as they occur, however their need to know is often low. Communicating to this group should be less frequent and more comprehensive. The best approach is often a weekly emailed status report. These reports are typically written by various project team leaders, providing a status on their respective areas of the project, then compiled, summarized, and emailed by the project manager. The overhead to the project is minimal and the depth of the communication satisfies even the most interested stakeholders.

Low/High (Interest/Power)

This group is often composed of busy executives that fall into the circle of control. They don't have the time, nor desire to meet face-to-face regarding a project, however they also do not want to be blind-sided. The best communication approach with this group is a brief phone call or voice mail message, referencing major accomplishments and/or significant issues and risks to the project. Follow this call with an email attaching the project's risk register and an offer to explain each risk in greater detail as required. The overhead is fairly significant with this group, but should be likened to paying an insurance premium.

Low/Low (Interest/Power)

This group should not be communicated to regarding the project. Many of the stakeholders in the circle of concern fall into this quadrant, thereby reducing the overall burden of communication. Some project managers feel they should communicate with all potential stakeholders, however this approach reduces focus and increases non-value add activities.

Communications Strategy

Converting a stakeholder analysis into an effective communications strategy requires a clear understanding of each stakeholder's WIFM. The strategy involves techniques in meeting as many, or all, of the WIFMs among the most important stakeholders. In practice, this means the project manager addresses the underlying motivations in face-to-face discussions, or when speaking over the phone. Each verbal communication becomes a custom delivery of facts packaged in such a way that the stakeholder feels his or her personal objectives are being met. This topic is quite complex when viewed through the lens of politics and justifies a book to address it in sufficient detail. For our purposes, understand that merely pushing out project information is an unsophisticated approach to communicating and does not accomplish higher-level goals of project management. Nevertheless, using the information gathered in the stakeholder analysis, a communications matrix can be developed, as depicted in Figure 4.3. This matrix serves as a game plan for the project manager to follow.

COMMUNICATIONS MATRIX

FIGURE 4.3

Stakeholder Name/Title/Group	Interest/Power Rating	Communication Type(s)	Communication Channel(s)	Communication Frequency	Special Considerations

Developing a communications matrix does not necessarily ensure that communication will actually occur during the lifecycle of the project. To translate intentions into reality, communications tasks and milestones should be added to the WBS, and resourced appropriately. The role of the project manager is said to consist of communication activities at least 80% of the time, so accounting for this time in the project schedule is significant. Integrating communications activities into the project plan is the sign of a seasoned project manager and a well planned project. Don't underestimate the importance of this process.

Project Politics

Another aspect of project communication involves the various political perspectives that affect the project environment: team, function, organizational, and external. To better understand a project's political environment, it's important to describe politics as:

1. Intrigue or maneuvering within a group in order to gain control or power
2. The often internally conflicting interrelationships among people in a company

These definitions help establish the boundaries of politics, which is often a very ambiguous term among project managers. Through identifying politics, it is possible to navigate successfully. Be careful to not automatically associate politics with unethical behavior. For some, the mere mention of the word politics is enough to make them shudder, with thoughts of "dirty politics" leaping immediately to mind. People who undermine decisions, by-pass procedure, and manipulate team members for self-serving purposes are the "dirty" politicians. Unfortunately, these are the people who most often come to mind when talking about politics.

Fortunately there is such as thing as “noble politics.” Politics is really about how you work with people. You can use political savvy and still be completely ethical and above-board. That's the kind of politics the project manager needs to focus on; where everyone wins. Politics in and of itself is not dirty, it can be used with either negative or noble intentions. There are those who help others to be successful, who pursue the goals of the team and the organization, and who build coalitions with clients and other members. These are the "noble" practitioners of politics. These are the people you want leading your projects. They are the people you will respect when the project is complete and the individuals you want to work with on future projects. There is no doubt that politics is vital to project success and that project managers need to practice “noble” politics. This can be achieved by aligning the team, functional areas, organizational and external stakeholder interests, and their respective WIFMs. Obviously this is easier said than done, however if there is a way to meet all the stakeholder’s WIFMs with a single project, then this is the pinnacle of project leadership.

Connector Stakeholders

Recent research of informal networks identified key individuals that serve as connectors between social networks. These networks, both inside and outside of companies, provide value by streamlining the process of sending and receiving information. Connectors serve as knowledge brokers, however don't expect them to be labeled on an organization chart. Most connectors fly under the formal radar screen, yet they are very well known behind the scenes.

If a connector can be identified early in the lifecycle of a project, then the project manager can leverage the power of their social networks to increase communication exponentially. By gaining favor with the connectors and meeting their WIFMs, project managers stand to gain a critical project endorsement, or possibly some inside information pertinent to the success of the project. Some view this technique as "playing politics," however there is nothing inherently underhanded in the activity. The concept is really quite simple and above board. Knowing that people in an organization view the lynchpin as a credible source of opinion, the project manager can exploit this by explaining the rationale of a particular project, thereby ensuring the information is accurate when shared throughout the informal network. If all people involved are working toward the best interests of the organization, then leveraging informal networks in this way is a positive political maneuver and one that should be encouraged. Innovation projects, in particular, should be leveraged in this way, as the findings from many minor experiments conducted in obscurity throughout an organization culminate into a complete market solution. Unfortunately the scientist and the project manager often operate in different professional networks. The good news is that there exist connectors in virtually every organization that join these two worlds, and many others. Connectors act as liaisons of ideas, interpreters of data, and brokers of information.

Trends in Communication

There are many new and exciting trends in communication with the merging of mobile devices into a single platform, however with regard to project management, there are three technologies that rise to the top. These are major productivity enhancers and communication boosters. First of all is the smart phone. This device has become a critical component to the life of a project manager as they migrate between meetings. Aside from the standard phone capabilities, what makes these units special are the Qwerty keyboard and Internet connection. In places where opening and using a laptop is not possible, or polite, a project manager can receive and respond to critical emails and pages. This device allows the project manager to bridge the gap between laptop usages, thereby placing communication back onto the radar screen. A second tool that is often under estimated is instant messaging

(IM). IM gets a bad rap due to its abuse in the workplace. This can be attributed to its ease of use and accessibility in many cases; the same attributes that make it such a powerful tool. Once project managers connect their team through IM, standard email seems prehistoric. The speed at which communication can occur using IM is exponentially faster than email, assuming emails are even read. IM interfaces let the project manager know who is online and who is not, as well as when a person is responding to a message. Plus, unlike email, IM can involve multiple parties communicating in parallel.

Finally, is the new video conferencing capability of telepresence. This new system makes traditional video conferencing seem like comparing 12" black and white televisions to 60" HDTV LCD displays, there's simply no comparison. Unfortunately, there are not many of these in use today due to their large price tag of several hundred thousand dollars each, plus a substantial monthly fee in the tens of thousands per system. As the technology becomes more mainstream and additional competitors enter the market, the price will surely drop. The essence of telepresence systems is that they create an environment where the people communicating feel they are in the same room together even though they may be on other sides of the world. Some of the major players in this market today are HP, Cisco, and Polycom, with many more to follow. When viewed as a corporate tool to reduce travel expenses, the ROI is certainly credible. As commercial air travel becomes more and more congested, companies will begin to view telepresence systems as alternatives to services such as Netjets. We will also likely see telepresence moving in the same direction as Netjets, where customers pay for a percentage of usage, rather than purchasing a complete system.

Risk Management

Risk management started in the financial world to minimize such things as insurance claim losses. It then evolved into a corporate enterprise tool, used in identifying such things as conformance to legal and regulatory policies, for example. However, today the focus of risk management is expanded considerably, to the point where it encompasses program and project risk. Whenever a degree of uncertainty exists, then risk management should be utilized. For example, while working on contract with AgustaWestlandBell, the recipient of the U.S. Presidential helicopter contract award in January 2005, I conducted what is known as enterprise risk management (ERM). ERM is focused on the operations of the corporate entity, rather than specific programs. For instance, our most critical consequence during the risk analysis phase of this effort was considered loss of contract to build Marine One. We looked at things like human resource processes, facility fire suppression systems, legal and financial policy, and the like. In parallel with this activity was another effort specifically focused on the development program of the helicopter itself. Known as program or project risk management, the types of things reviewed were more engineering and logistics related. For purposes of this book, our discussion on risk management will be focused on programs and projects, not corporate enterprises.

Managing project risks is critically important when dealing with innovation projects in particular, given their characteristically high uncertainty. In fact, some could argue that this one activity represents the largest lever a pro-active project manager has in keeping innovation project on track. Unlike low-risk projects with standard task durations based on historical data, innovation projects typically have very dynamic schedules and budgets. From a management perspective, risk represents what is unknown on a project. As the project unfolds and more information is gained, then obviously the percent of unknown information goes down. Good project managers look into the future at the sea of unknown and then navigate their projects toward experiments that will yield the greatest amount of learning in the shortest amount of time. Navigating the entire sea of unknown information is impossible for most projects, therefore selecting which tides to take advantage of can make the difference between success and failure. The other, somewhat smaller, lever that a project manager can exercise is the learning-cycle lever, or the rate-of-speed at which learning occurs. You could say that navigating to the best learning spots in the sea of unknown information and then maximizing the speed by which those spots are understood is the essence of how innovation project managers add value. It's a simple concept to understand, but much more difficult to put into action. To ease in this transition to being a manager of risk and an enabler of innovation, it is critical that the project manager knows what risks are and what they are not.

Understanding risk management requires a clear definition of the characteristics of a risk. First of all, risks are not problems and they are not necessarily issues; risks are future events that have less than a 100% probability of occurring. Unlike risks, problems have a 100% likelihood of occurrence and simply need to be solved. Figure 4.4 depicts a decision making process to help distinguish risks from problems and issues.

RISK IDENTIFICATION FLOWCHART

FIGURE 4.4

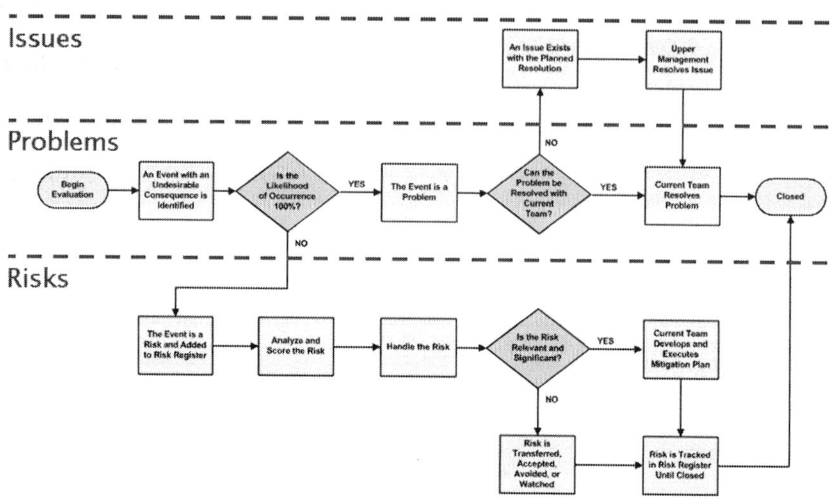

Identify the Risks

Once you know what a risk looks like, it's necessary to go out and find them, but don't make the mistake that many inexperienced project managers make by working in isolation. It's prudent to personally come up with a draft list of risks as a starting point in the project, however proper risk management requires a series of interviews with subject-matter experts who are associated with the project. When interviewing, the first step is to ask about the things that worry the interviewees. Questions like, "so, what aspects of this project are you most worried about?" are open ended and can elucidate additional items to probe. After capturing as many of the high-level worries as possible, the next step is to dig deeper into each worry by breaking each one down into singular events, causes, and consequences. It is also important that each risk statement is formulated according to the same structure, thereby enabling an apples to apples comparison. A common approach to formulating the risk statement is:

"If event happens due to cause then undesirable consequences may occur."

When interviewing for risks, there are various techniques that a project manager can use to drill down to the root causes, such as the "five whys" technique, which as the title suggests, involves asking "why" until a single primary cause has been reached. It is also necessary to question the consequences until they truly affect the most important project requirements, which in the case of innovation is typically rate-of-learning. Some textbooks on risk management also encourage the identification of opportunities during the risk identification process, however this can become confusing when scoring risks, as we will cover later in this Chapter. One technique is to document an opportunity by creating a risk statement that is the antithesis of the opportunity statement. For example, if the following opportunity has been identified:

Using carbon matrix composite materials will give us a major weight savings for our jet engine program, thereby increasing fuel efficiency and the thrust-to-weight ratio.

Then a risk statement can be formulated that will encourage this opportunity. For example:

If weight reduction cannot be achieved on the jet engine program due to the insufficiency of carbon matrix composite materials then we will not be able to meet our fuel efficiency and thrust-to-weight ratio targets.

Using this strategy allows all risks and opportunities to be analyzed and handled using the same process, which is much simpler to manage.

Analyze the Risks

When analyzing risk statements, there are three primary areas upon which the consequences are relevant: schedule, budget, and performance. Risks typically affect one or more of these areas and should be classified accordingly. This is important during the risk scoring process, where criteria for each area will be used to evaluate the risk statement. The risk areas are more or less self explanatory; events that could move out the date at which the project is delivered are schedule risks, events that could cause the budget to increase are budget risks, and events that could reduce the functionality, or scope of the project, are performance risks. This classification may make more sense after reviewing the example risk-register depicted in Figure 4.5.

RISK-REGISTER

FIGURE 4.5

Risk ID	P/C/S	Risk Statement	Risk Rating			Mitigation	Owner Name	Modified	Estimated Due Date
			L	C	S				
001	P	IF... BECAUSE... THEN...	5	4		WE WILL DO XYZ...	Jane Deere	MM/DD/YY	MM/DD/YY
002			4	3	12				
003			3	2	[illegible]				
004			0	0					
005			0	0					
006			0	0					
007			0	0					
008			0	0					
009			0	0					
010			0	0					
011			0	0					

As you can see in reviewing the risk-register example, there are columns to capture the risk statement, the areas the risk may affect, the likelihood and consequence scores of the risk, the handling strategy, and finally the risk owner. Before we go further in learning how to score a risk, we must first learn how to build a custom risk-register for a business.

Defining Risk Scales

The scales you define for your risk-register should be based on the level of granularity by which you plan to identify risks. Most large projects will tend to have several hundred risks, where small projects may only have a dozen. The lower the number of risks you may have, the more granular you may want to design your risk-register. For example, NASA uses a 5x5 matrix to capture its program risks, which are quite extensive as you can imagine. Smaller organizations may choose more granularity, such as a 10x10 matrix. Figure 4.6 depicts an example of a 5x5 matrix currently used by NASA.

RISK SCORING MATRIX

FIGURE 4.6

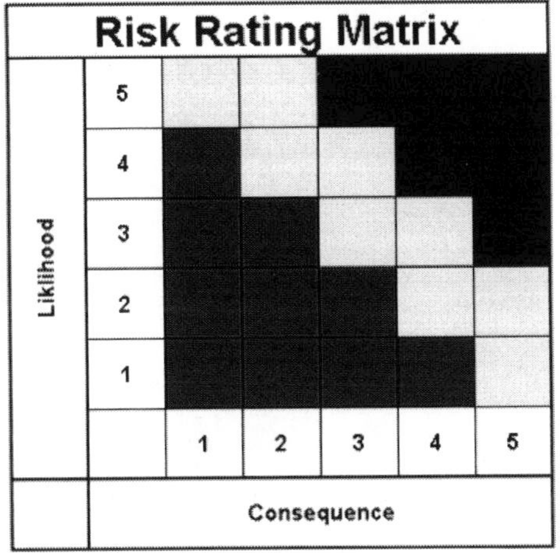

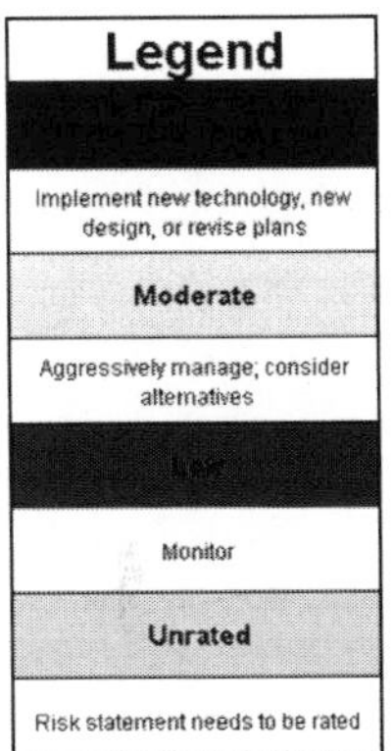

Likelihood scales are relatively simple to define. The largest weighting (in this case a 5) should be assigned to the lowest likelihood of event prevention based on the existing project plan. In other words, a likelihood score of 5 should be associated with events that will most likely happen. Another way of differentiating likelihood scores is by percentage of probability. For example, a likelihood score of 5 could be associated with events that have greater than a 90% chance of occurring, a likelihood score of 1 could be associated with events that have less than a 10% chance of occurring, and so forth.

Similarly, consequence scales should be designed according to the size of a project. Using a five point scale is recommended, however this can be adjusted as discussed earlier. A very important aspect of this activity is the definition of the various consequence ranges based on the requirements of your project. See Figure 4.7 for an example of definitions for likelihood and consequence categories applicable for many innovation oriented projects.

RISK LIKELIHOOD AND CONSEQUENCE
FIGURE 4.7

Consequence	Level	1	2	3	4	5
	Process Performance	Minimal or nc impact	Minor shortfal; same approach	Moderate shortfall have alternatives	Unacceptable; have alternatives	Unacceptable; no alternatives exist
	Cost		Increase < 5%	Increase >= 5%	Increase >= 7%	Increase >= 10%
	Schedule		Additional activities can meet date	Minor schedule slip; will miss need date	Program critical path impacted	Cannot achieve key program milestones

Liklihood	Level	The current plan...
	5	...cannot prevent this event; no alternatives are available.
	4	...cannot prevent this event; alternatives are available.
	3	...may prevent this event, but additional actions will be required.
	2	...is usually sufficient to prevent this type of event.
	1	...is sufficient to prevent this event.

Scoring Risks

Once your risk statements have been captured and a customized risk-register has been developed, then it's time to score the risks.

First, examine each risk to isolate the cause and determine the likelihood and consequences based on your pre-defined definitions in the risk-register. Assess each risk and then be sure to analyze the integrated risk environment, which basically means identifying the risks inherent in the relationships between the individual risks. In other words, there are positive, negative, and inverse correlations between the risks that must be accounted for. Analyzing these relationships takes experience, judgment, and much trial and error, but over time trends will begin to emerge.

Risk Handling Strategies

Most people assume that risks are automatically mitigated. This is only partially true. Project managers actually have several ways to reduce risks to acceptable levels, such as by watching, transferring, accepting, avoiding, or mitigating. Some people think that contingency plans are mitigation strategies, but they are actually no more than risk acceptance strategies. When choosing which handling approach to apply to a particular risk, much of the decision relies on the total score of the risk itself. Low scoring risks, or green risks, should be watched. The benefit of mitigating a green risk is often less than the cost associated with the mitigation activity, therefore it makes little sense to go down this path. Scarce resources should be deployed on reducing the potential impact of the highest scored and most critical risks. Transferring risks is a viable strategy when dealing with suppliers or partners that are responsible for the part of the project associated with a particular risk. Asking the supplier or partner to handle a risk they control is a great way to spread accountability across a project. Accepting a risk occurs when the total score is in a range that does not warrant a risk reduction activity. Many medium, or yellow-risks, fall into this category. Some risks can also be avoided completely by simply choosing a different supplier, or selecting an alternate material. If several options are available to fulfill a particular aspect of your project, then choose the one with the lowest risk when possible. The most time intensive activity in risk management is risk mitigation. Keep in mind that only a small percentage of risks will ever be mitigated. Usually all high, or red risk, will end up having some type of mitigation strategy. Mitigation means the likelihood and consequence profile of a risk will be reduced to an acceptable level by initiating a focused activity.

Risk Planning

Project managers should constantly evaluate a project's total risk profile and work toward keeping it in an acceptable range. Savvy project managers realize that managing and mitigating risk takes time and resources, therefore they account for this overhead burden in their project's schedules and budgets. Tasks associated with the risk management process should be added to the WBS, with resources assigned to the various activities. Reviewing the risk-register should be a continual process for the project manager and a routine process for the project team. A good practice is to get the entire project team together once per week to review the risk-register, status mitigation activities, add new risks, and re-score risks that have been handled. If you haven't gatherer it yet, the risk-register is considered a living document, therefore using a web enabled system to store risk information is optimal, thereby allowing all team members to have access to real-time information continually. It's also wise to review the risk-register with a project's sponsor on a periodic basis. This is often a good way to gather external and environmental risks not readily apparent to the project team. Communicating project risks broadly often exposes unintended impacts, as well as allows the project team to exploit the collective experience of the organization.

Managing Risks on Innovation Projects

One of the tricky aspects of risk management on innovation projects is that everything is typically scored as a high risk. Due to the high degree of uncertainty, the approach the project manager takes when identifying risks is critical. Most research and development engineers, for example, will claim that they cannot know the likelihood and consequences of experimental activities, since there is no historical data to rely on when evaluating. In these cases, the project manager needs to help the engineer think through the various options associated with solving a particular problem. One way to do this effectively is to capture the discussion on a whiteboard. Start by listing all of the project's objectives horizontally along the top of the whiteboard, then identify all of the working theories, or approaches, the engineer feels are viable in seeking solutions to the objectives. List the working theories as bullet items under each respective objective. Then under each bulleted working theory, ask the engineer to identify the hypothesis, or experiments, that they plan to test to better understand each working theory. What will result is a portfolio of planned experiments grouped under working theories devised to meet the project's objectives. See Figure 4.8 for a depiction of this approach to gathering innovation risks.

INNOVATION RISK DIAGRAM

FIGURE 4.8

RESEARCH OBJECTIVE 1		
Working Theory 1	Hypothesis/Experiment A	Relationship/Dependencies
	Hypothesis/Experiment B	Relationship/Dependencies
	Hypothesis/Experiment C	Relationship/Dependencies
Working Theory 2	Hypothesis/Experiment D	Relationship/Dependencies
	Hypothesis/Experiment E	Relationship/Dependencies
	Hypothesis/Experiment F	Relationship/Dependencies
Working Theory 3	Hypothesis/Experiment G	Relationship/Dependencies
	Hypothesis/Experiment H	Relationship/Dependencies
	Hypothesis/Experiment I	Relationship/Dependencies

After identifying the portfolio of experiments, the project manager can then begin the scoring process by asking the engineer a series of probing questions, such as:

What is the likelihood that your planned experiment will not result in a better understanding of your working theory?

If your planned experiment does not further your understanding of your working theory, what are the consequences to the project's schedule, budget, and/or performance?

Engineers often refer to the results of their experiments as toggling. The results can positively or negatively toggle the factors in the hypothesis, meaning the hypothesis is proven right or wrong. In either case, the engineer has learned from the experiment, therefore the activity was valuable to the project. However, some experiments do not toggle any of the factors. In these cases, the learning process has not been advanced and the time and cost associated with the experiment was a waste. In many cases, this situation arises when experiments are designed poorly. Obviously, this is an area that must be measured and minimized to ensure a high rate-of-learning. The primary purpose of risk management on innovation projects is to help identify the highest scored experiments and then mitigate these by either redesigning the experiments to achieve a toggle, or bundling them with similar, albeit lower scored experiments. Using risk management in this manner will help speed up the rate-of-learning and ensure resources are applied to the most valuable activities.

Chapter 5

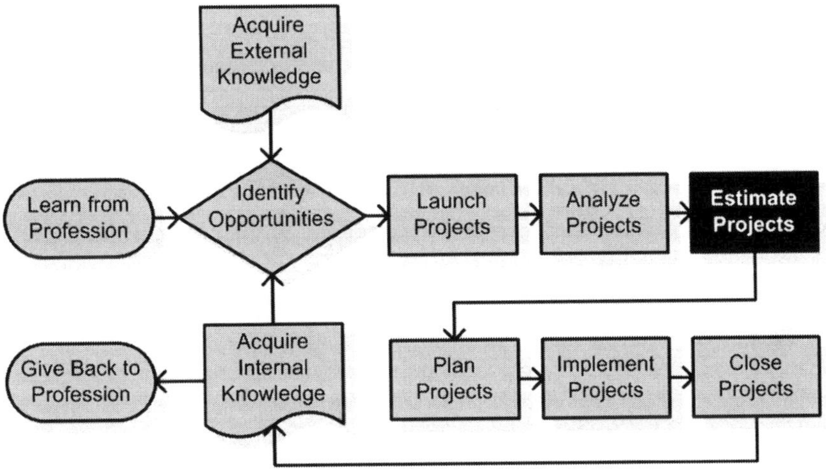

Estimating Schedule and Cost

After an opportunity is selected and chartered as an approved project, the communications plan is developed, and the initial pass at risk planning is complete, the project team is ready to estimate the schedule and cost of the project. The primary purpose of this phase of the process is to produce a specific project duration and cost target. Both will have boundaries of uncertainty that create a range of potential duration and cost targets from earliest delivery date and lowest cost to worst case. It's important to develop these ranges for future negotiations with the project's sponsor when establishing congruency among the triple-constraints. This topic will be covered in greater detail in Chapter 6.

Creating the Work Breakdown Structure

A WBS is basically an outline of the project's high-level tasks. To effectively structure the WBS, the project team must think through the logical sequence of activities and potential groupings of related tasks before committing to a document. Brainstorming with the team using a whiteboard is one effective way to quickly capture and iterate on input. Start with the biggest chunks of the project first. For example, if your project was to develop and implement a knowledge management system, the major areas might involve application design, application development, application testing, application deployment, and end user training. These five major chunks form the first-level of the project's outline. The project team then elaborates on the second level activities within each major chuck. If we fleshed out the application design chuck, it might include requirements gathering, functional specification development, architecture design, and a user interface mock-up. These four chunks form the second-level of the project's outline and the umbrella statements for more discrete tasks. Figure 5.1 depicts an example of a WBS for a knowledge management system.

WORK BREAKDOWN STRUCTURE

FIGURE 5.1

WORK BREAKDOWN STRUCTURE (WBS)		
	Requirements Gathering	
		Task 1 - Duration
		Task 2 - Duration
		Task 3 - Duration
	Functional Specification Development	
		Task 1 - Duration
Application Design		Task 2 - Duration
		Task 3 - Duration
	Architecture Design	
		Task 1 - Duration
		Task 2 - Duration
		Task 3 - Duration
	User Interface Mock-Up	
		Task 1 - Duration
		Task 2 - Duration
		Task 3 - Duration
Application Development		
Application Testing		
Application Deployment		
End User Training		

Knowing when to stop outlining a project is just as important as the content that you add. Too high-level of a WBS will not provide sufficient detail to make informed duration estimates, while too much detail becomes overwhelming on large projects and causes resources to be scheduled by the hour, instead of day or week. In traditional project management methodologies, project teams continue deconstructing the project until they reach a level of activity granularity where status and completion can be measured. Known as tasks at this level in the WBS, they are bounded with a clear beginning and ending point, they have clear deliverables, and duration and resource hours can be estimated.

This approach works well for traditional projects, but not necessarily innovation projects. The issue on innovation projects is that the tasks are often unknown. For example, when developing a new semiconductor process, the engineer knows that he will need to formulate and run experiments to characterize various process steps, but is not sure of the number and type of experiments that will be required to gain process maturity. In these cases, the project manager is better off defining the various defects, or issues the engineer needs to characterize, then establishing the average number of experimental cycles required to solve each issue based on the given complexity of the issue. In this way, the project manager can establish experimental boundaries that the engineer must try to work within. If a particular issue cannot be fully understood within the allotted time, then the hypothesis may need to be examined, as well as the approach. Running more experiments under the same hypothesis may not yield the toggles required to mature the process.

The bottom line is that a WBS should be sufficiently fleshed out to allow the project manager to input the tasks into a scheduling engine, such as Microsoft's Project application, having single owners and durations with the precision of days.

Work Packages

Grouping related tasks together in your WBS not only helps in logically understanding the flow of the project, but also makes outsourcing chucks of activities much easier, if that route is taken. When organizing your WBS, the project manager should think about the parts of the project that could be done faster and cheaper by an external vendor. High-risk components of a project should also be grouped in this way, as outsourcing them allows the project manager to transfer the risks to the vendor. The level of effort in this scenario switches from task management to contract management. When selecting which parts of a project to outsource, consider activities that are routine, high-risk, or require significant capital investment to accomplish. Common outsourced work packages are software development, industrial manufacturing, and most aspects of construction projects. In fact, most construction projects deal more with procurement management and contract management than project management due to the large percentage of the work that is distributed to general contractors and service providers. To help in selecting what activities to outsource, a project manager may consider the model depicted in Figure 5.2.

FRONT-ROOM/BACK-ROOM DIAGRAM
FIGURE 5.2

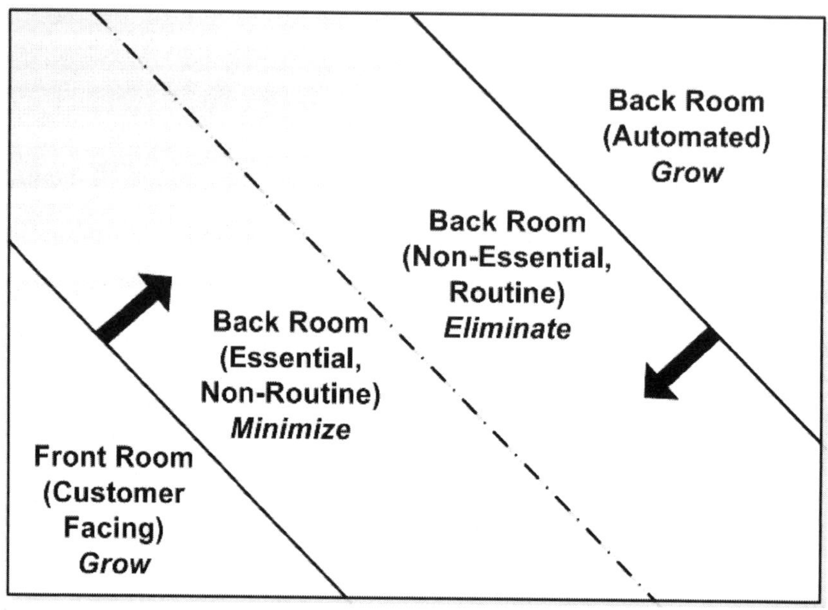

According to this model, customer facing activities, or the front-room, should be completed by project team members employed by the parent company. This would include requirements gathering, customer presentations, voice of the customer activities, and the like. All other activities fall into the non-customer facing group, or back-room. Within the back-room categories, three distinctions exist: essential activities, non-essential activities, and repetitive activities. The challenge that managers have is to increase the number of customer facing activities, while decreasing the number of essential activities, outsourcing non-essential activities, and automating all repetitive tasks through software or robotics. Front-room/back-room forces businesses to focus on their customers, while also driving low cost and responsive operations into the culture.

Communication and Risk Tasks

Tasks that often do not make there way into the WBS are those discussed in Chapter 4, namely communication and risk related activities. Many inexperienced project managers figure they will add these activities into the project within the pockets of time in the project plan, known as slack. They don't take into consideration the critical path activities that will consume the bulk of their time and, by definition, have no slack to play with. The result is often a poorly executed communications plan and a disregard for project risks. In other words, the project spirals out of control, causing confusion among the stakeholders and firefighting among the project team members. To avoid this state of chaos, project managers must include task statements in the WBS that carve out time for communication activities and risk handling activities. For example, if part of your communications plan includes daily one hour meetings with the project team to review status, yet this activity is not accounted for in the plan, then project team members will either work overtime to get their other scheduled tasks completed, or more likely, the project will simply get extended, thereby causing a missed delivery date. Likewise, if risk handling activities are not accounted for, project team members will either work overtime or ignore the activities completely. In the case of overtime, many states require a company to pay 1.5 times the hourly rate, leading to major project cost overruns. If overtime pay is not required, projects will still suffer as overworked team members become lethargic and jaded. To be sure, a little task planning upfront by the project manager can avoid a lot of problems down the road.

Rough Order of Magnitude Estimating

When initially estimating the durations of tasks it is likely that more information will be required to fully understand the driving factors affecting level of effort. Investigating tasks to this level of detail can take more time than is available or necessary. To continue with the estimating task and meet the needs of the project plan at this stage of development, the project team should develop what is known as rough order of magnitude estimates, or ROM estimates. ROM estimates provide an estimation range which is reflective of the uncertainty associated with the initial understanding of the project tasks. To gain a more accurate nominal estimate of each task, taking into consideration the range of uncertainty and the probabilities of the ROM estimate, the project manager should utilize the following formula:

ROM Duration Estimate = (Best Case + 4 x Nominal + Worst Case)/6,

where Best Case = -25% of Nominal and Worst Case = +75% of Nominal

By using this formula, the project manager can confidently discuss project durations having factored in uncertainty and probabilities. This first pass at developing task-level duration estimates will eventually be used to determine the total estimated work package durations, as well as the total duration for the project. In Chapter 6 we will discuss the methodology used to develop a more precise duration estimate before baselining the project plan.

Task Sequencing and Dependencies

We've discussed the process of outlining a project to create a WBS and providing enough task granularity to allow duration estimates to be made. We reviewed the purpose of developing work packages by grouping related tasks into discrete bundles that can be outsourced. We covered the importance of including communication and risk related tasks in the WBS to ensure we produce a plan that is reflective of reality. Finally, we reviewed the formulas required to develop a ROM duration estimate for each task, which will eventually be used to estimate the duration for the entire project. Next, we will review the process of task sequencing based on dependencies between the tasks. The first step in this process is to gain a rough understanding of the logical order by which all the work packages should be completed, with the earliest at the top of the list, followed by the next in sequential order, and so forth. Once this is complete, the tasks within each work package should be ordered in the same way. Finally, the dependencies between tasks should be considered in performing a second round of ordering. Fortunately, much of this effort of assigning and managing dependencies can be accomplished using a scheduling engine, such as Microsoft's Project application.

Scheduling Engines

Project management software has made the life of project managers much easier, enabling the automation of many manual activities, including the linking of dependent tasks and assigning of resources. This book will not cover the functionality of specific project management applications, since that level of information could fill a book of its own. We will discuss, however, the best use of these types of systems when managing innovation projects. A common mistake made by many inexperienced project managers is to try to account for every hour of every team members day for the entire project. These project managers detail every task within a scheduling engine and waste many hours estimating each low-level task with excruciating precision. These same project managers then transform into task-masters as they micro-manage every decision and every activity of the team. It doesn't take a rocket scientist to see why this is not a sustainable practice, not to mention how it completely squashes innovation.

The better way to develop a schedule for innovation projects is to start by entering the information contained in the WBS into the scheduling engine, then highlight natural milestones within the schedule where interim deliverables are due, certain data is required, or where key decisions must be made. It's often helpful to perform this analysis with the Gantt view of the schedule. If you choose to integrate phased-gate development milestones into your project schedule, these can also be entered into the application at this time and can serve as a framework for the other project specific milestones. Enter in all the tasks, ROM duration estimates, and dependencies into the scheduling engine. Using the functionality of the scheduling engine, generate the critical path of the project, which is the series of tasks that are dependent on one another and establish the total duration of the project. All other tasks not on the critical path have what is known as slack time. In other words, non-critical path tasks can start late and end late up to the amount of slack time they contain before affecting the critical path of the project. Understanding the concept of the critical path is particularly important for project managers of innovation projects. The critical path tasks are the ones that the project manager should track and status, while monitoring other tasks from a distance. The challenge comes during the execution of the project, as the critical path becomes a moving target, often changing as tasks are completed and schedule dates are modified. By following this approach, project managers can focus on risk management; keeping track of events that may affect the critical path. This involves new tasks entering the critical path, as well as tasks exiting. Keeping an eye on meeting the end delivery date, while managing risk around the critical path, positions the project manager as a conductor of an orchestra of creative project activities, rather than bureaucratic administrator of mindless tasks. Innovators need to know the problem they need to solve and the date the solution is required to feed the next phase of the project, but not how to go about developing a solution.

Determining Total Project Duration and Cost

Using the functionality of a scheduling engine to develop a project's critical path is the only simple method of determining the total estimated duration of a project. If the ROM duration estimates were used when adding the tasks to the scheduling engine, then the uncertainty boundary of the project will be rolled up in the total duration. This piece of information is one of the key items that will be negotiated with the project sponsor when working toward congruency of the triple-constraints of the project. The other two, of course, are scope and cost. To uncover the total estimated project cost, the scheduling engine will once again be utilized, but only for labor costs. To accomplish this step, the project manager should establish labor categories, with associated burden rates for each. Burden rates can be computed by dividing an average salary by 2080 hours, then adding the hourly ratio of allocated overhead, which is typically sales, general, and administrative expenses. Project sponsors would likely fall into the category of a senior executive, while project team members might be considered individual contributors. A range of labor categories with associated burden rates included may be as follows:

- *Senior Executive* *($300.00/hour)*
- *Senior Manager* *($175.00/hour)*
- *Project Manager* *($125.00/hour)*
- *Senior Engineer* *($100.00/hour)*
- *Individual Contributor* *($70.00/hour)*
- *Administrative Support* *($35.00/hour)*

By adding a predefined labor category with associated labor rate to each task in the scheduling engine, the project manager can quickly roll up the estimated costs of the project. At this point in the estimation, it's easier to make some general assumptions, such as resources will be working an eight hour day, five days per week. Also, assume full-time effort on a task as it is estimated, rather than breaking resource efforts into percentage of time allocated. Critical path tasks should be scrutinized in greater detail, of course, but overall, this approach will provide a good estimate of a project without the need for very time consuming analysis of all of the tasks.

Final Cost Considerations

Using the aforementioned methodology, the project manager can derive an estimated labor cost required to complete the project. However, there are other costs that must be calculated, such as capital purchases, materials, leases, and the like. Like the WBS, these expenses can be inputted in a scheduling engine, however experience has proven that using a spreadsheet, such as MS Excel, is the best approach. To determine the total estimated cost of a project using a spreadsheet, simply enter in the labor cost that was generated by the scheduling engine, then list out all the anticipated purchases that the project will require, such as machinery, furniture, tooling, etc. Also list any one time and recurring expenses the project may generate, such as software purchases, office lease agreements, subject-matter expert contract fees, and so forth. One additional item to add to the budget, which is often overlooked, is known as the management reserve. The management reserve typically consists of a fund made up of 10% of the total project cost set aside to allow the project manager to handle unexpected risks that arise during the execution of the project. At the end of a project, whatever funds are remaining are returned to the project's sponsor with a full accounting of how the money was used.

Chapter 6

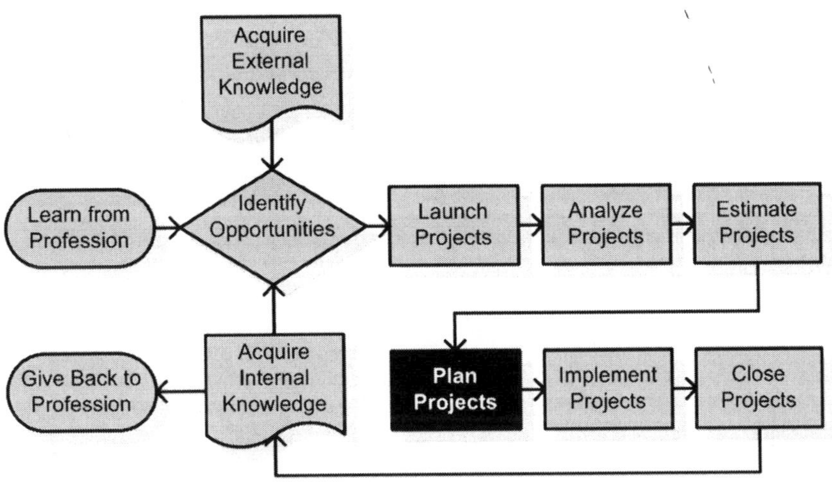

Baselining the Triple-Constraint

The triple-constraint is the essence of project management and what a project manager must identify and maintain. The steps covered in prior Chapters of this book describe how to develop each constraint of the triple-constraint: scope, schedule, and budget. However, identifying these constraints is only half of the process, and not nearly as important as establishing congruency between the three. To understand this concept, we must first define congruence as the degree to which factors agree, or coincide with one another. A state of agreement between the scope, schedule, and budget simply means that the level of functionality, or end result defined by the scope document can be successfully delivered within the time allotted in the schedule and the cost allotted in the budget. It's helpful to think of each of the triple-constraints as a side of a triangle with the length of each side loosely corresponding in length to the constraint's contribution to the project. The area within the triangle represents the area of congruence as depicted in Figure 6.1.

TRIPLE-CONSTRAINT DIAGRAM
FIGURE 6.1

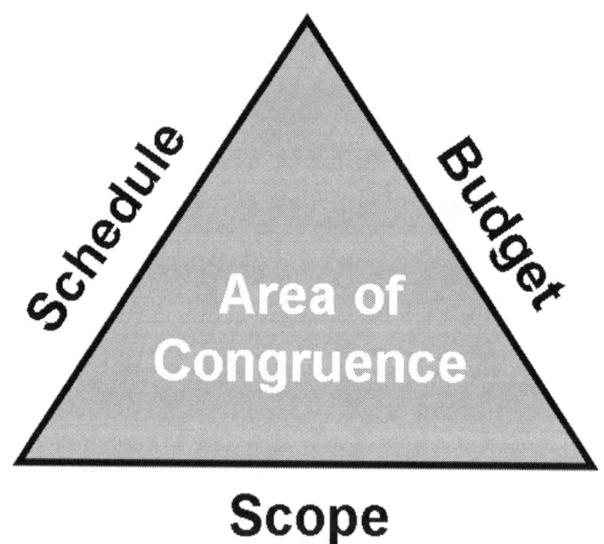

When a project becomes baselined, it means the project sponsor has agreed to accepting the results spelled out in the scope document within the time defined in the schedule and for the amount of money indicated in the budget. The project manager's job is to ensure that the project can be successfully delivered based on the agreement, or that the triple-constraint defined in the project plan is congruent. The degree to which the triple-constraint is congruent defines the quality of the project plan. In other words, a perfectly planned project would have its schedule, scope, and budget perfectly congruent.

Establishing congruency of the triple-constraint is required before a project plan can become baselined and the implementation can begin. However, this important step in the project does not happen by chance, it requires negotiation with the project's sponsor.

Negotiating the Triple-Constraint

Every project is born from a problem that needs to be solved. The person that has the greatest vested interest in ensuring the problem is solved typically becomes the project's sponsor. The sponsor further defines the problem to be solved, then charters a project and assigns a project manager to develop the solution. The project manager then articulates the approach he or she will take in solving the problem, hence the scope document is created. From this scope document, the project manager estimates the time and cost required to successfully deliver the solution. It is at this point that the project manager must return to the sponsor and negotiate the three elements that have been created: scope, schedule, and budget. The preliminary scope document typically contains everything the project sponsor would want in a product, service, or result, assuming time and cost were of no consequence. This is a view of the project in a perfect world, so to speak. Unfortunately, very few projects exist in a perfect world, therefore negotiation must take place. When a sponsor is faced with the reality of how long a project will take to complete, as well as the cost required, they are usually willing to give up on some of the aspects of the scope to bring one or more of these factors into check. It's the project manager's responsibility to walk the sponsor through a tradeoff analysis of what they can expect in a solution if they pull in the schedule or reduce the budget. The project manager acts as a salesperson, explaining the cost/benefit of various decisions the sponsor must make until they ultimately arrive at a project scope that satisfies the most important aspects of the problem, while meeting a schedule and budget that is satisfactory to the sponsor. When agreement is reached with the sponsor and the project manager feels that the project can be successful, then congruency has been reached. At this point, the project manager is justified in spending the time to further define the project plan.

Triple-Constraint

To baseline a triple-constraint simply means the scope, schedule, and budget have become the initial contract by which the team will work toward fulfilling. Before baselining can occur, however, the project manager must fine-tune his estimates of the schedule and budget. The initial ROM estimates must be replaced with more precise predictions. Rather than a range of -25% and +75% of the nominal, the estimates must fall within +/-10% of nominal. To achieve this level of precision, the project team needs to fully flesh out each of the tasks in the scheduling engine by assigning actual people to complete the work, instead of labor categories. Once the people are assigned, it is their responsibility to analyze their tasks and develop a precise estimate of the time it will take them to complete the work. Their estimate should fall within the initial uncertainty boundary of -25% - +75% as originally defined. Therefore a precise project duration and cost estimate will always be less than the ROM estimates agreed to by the sponsor, thereby creating a positive mood for all involved.

The Project Plan

Before a project team can begin the work of executing the tasks of a project, an approved project plan must be available. This is the first major deliverable of a project team and a significant milestone in a project's lifecycle. We say that a project plan is baselined when the project sponsor has signed off on the revised definition of the project scope and precise estimates of the schedule and budget. Also included in this plan is the communication plan and the risk management plan for the project. Many project management books will also suggest the inclusion of configuration control plans, implementation plans, as well as a cornucopia of other governing plans, however these documents are better established as a business process for all projects, as opposed to a specific element of a given project. In other words, governing procedures should be established at a corporate-level and be applied to all project activities. They should not be customized for each project and included as part of the project plan.

At the point that a project plan is approved and ready to implement, the project manager should hold a kickoff meeting by including all of the stakeholders in the circle of control and review each of the elements of the plan in detail. By the end of the meeting, everyone involved with the project should know exactly what problem they will be solving, the approach the project team will take to solve the problem, the work breakdown of the project, the schedule, budget, communications that can be expected, and the general profile of risks associated with the project. Getting everyone on the same page is the primary goal of this meeting, as well as establishing a transition from planning the project to implementing the project. Regarding project kickoff meetings, the project manager should focus on providing an overview of the project by covering the elements in the project scope document, address some of the relational aspects of the project team, as well as other dynamics associated with the greater stakeholder population. Finally, and probably most important, the project manager should set the pace and tone for the project team to emulate, set expectations for team members, and any protocols that should be followed, such as sick days, travel, and the like.

Kickoff meetings should be an exciting event where people eager to implement a solution to a pressing problem come together to join forces. The spirit of the meeting should be collegial and supportive, not directive and authoritarian. Project stakeholders should leave the meeting feeling informed and empowered to make decisions that will further the objectives and success of the project. Project managers should use the opportunity to establish a sense of rapport with each of the attendees and ensure that ambiguity is squeezed out of the collective minds of the group. This is accomplished through an open dialogue around the facets of the project plan. Simply expressing how things will happen will not elicit the breadth of questions that is required to reduce uncertainty.

Creating a Shared Vision

The most successful project are delivered by project teams that truly believe in the cause of the project and feel personally responsible for its successful outcome. Buying into a shared vision by the project team is critical to achieving their highest levels of performance. The project manager must provide the team with something to believe in. For a vision to be shared it must be able to be communicated, challenging, yet realistic, the project manager must believe in the vision and be passionate about it, and it should inspire others to participate and contribute.

An additional aspect of formulating a compelling vision is the development is an inspiring project slogan. A project slogan should encapsulate the value the project will deliver to the sponsor and the company. It should be clearly understood, simple, and inspiring.

Chapter 7

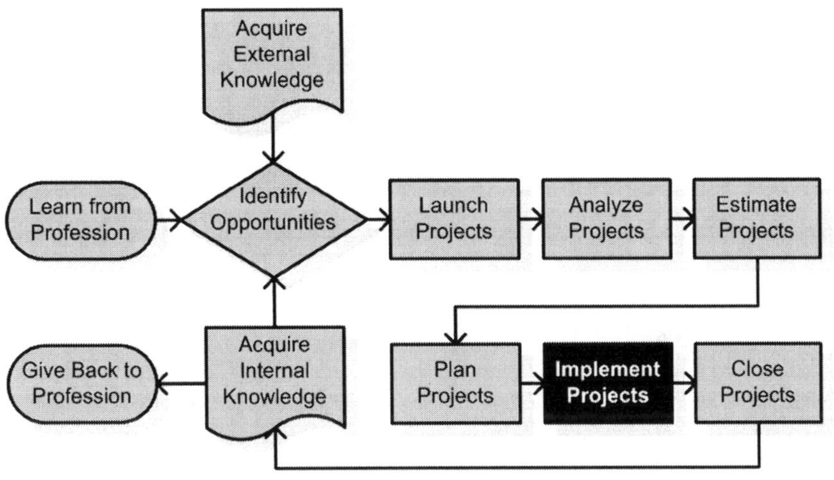

Managing Progressive Elaboration

Innovation projects require a new perspective on project management. The traditional approach to simply managing tasks is no longer sufficient. Instead, what should be managed are the learning process and the risk profile of the project. Due primarily to the high degree of uncertainty, but also to the inherent autonomy of knowledge workers, innovation projects but be facilitated more than managed. In fact, it would not be inappropriate to view the role of the project manager as part facilitator and part administrator. But like any good facilitation, the facilitator must understand the intended outcome and drive the activity toward meeting that objective.

Managing Project Learning

There are three primary components to the learning process: the rate-of-learning, the number of cycles-of-learning, and the quality of learning; each must be managed effectively to ensure the proper outcome. As stated earlier in this book, the project manager of innovation projects must set boundaries for innovation to occur, but cannot dictate the innovation process. Unlike traditional projects, innovation project are not usually linear in their progression. In fact, the paradox of learning is that it can occur without measurable progress occurring. By learning what doesn't work, an engineer can come closer to a solution even though they have nothing to show for it. This is why we count both positives and false-positives as learning opportunities in experimentation. This phenomena can be depicted in the yield curve of a typical innovation. Rather than a linear progression of the development of a solution, the innovation yield curve is typically flat for an extended period of time, then rockets up to a total solution represented by a steeply sloped yield curve. The speed at which an innovation comes to fruition is a component of all the smaller learning opportunities that led up to the final discovery. One of the project manager's responsibilities is to help facilitate this process by ensuring as many obstacles are removed from the process as possible. Maximizing the rate-of-learning can be accomplished by minimizing the bureaucracy that the innovator has to deal with, as well as getting the analysis of experimental results back to the innovator as quickly as possible. This sometimes means the project manager must act as a business process analyst, dissecting the overall learning process to ensure efficiency. Being proactive in this regard often pays enormous dividends in delivering project success. Since innovation cannot be placed in a box, it must be given the room and time required to blossom. Big insights often occur when our minds are thinking of other topics, or involved in deep quiet reflection. Innovation can incubate in our subconscious minds while we sleep, or take a walk, but innovation can not typically be forced to develop as if it were some sort of planned activity. The mysterious part of the process of innovation is that moment in time when the subconscious idea become a conscious thought that can be acted upon.

Cycles-of-learning is the second component to the innovation process that must be managed. This involves the number of learning opportunities that the innovator has available. For example, if the project manager determines that a solution to a problem must be delivered within three months to feed the next phase of a project, the innovator must plan their experiments to fit within the constraints of their environment, namely capacity and throughput. In the case of a semiconductor process innovation, an engineer may have twenty experiments that they would like to run to characterize a particular process step. Assuming the engineer had three months to produce a working process step, they would be forced to rank order the twenty experiments and only run those that fit within the constraints of the environment. If they chose to run a single lot of silicon wafers per experiment and the manufacturing facility had capacity to run three lots per month with a thirty-day throughput time per lot, the engineer would have to understand the relationship between the experiments and how the expected learning would affect the design of later experiments. Using a design of experiments approach, the engineer can establish the intended sequential learning opportunities that will best achieve the desired outcome. Under this scenario, the engineer would be able to characterize nine aspects of the process step from the total list of twenty they originally had. The project manager can help improve this situation by trying to increase the number of cycles-of-learning that can occur within the three month period of time.

Finally, quality of learning must be monitored by the project manager. This can be accomplished by facilitating the design of experiments and providing training where necessary. Experiments that are overly complex, or stacked on one another can become confounded, thereby eliminating the learning opportunity for the engineer. When variables that are being characterized, by relating their existence with a positive or negative correlation with observable phenomena, cannot be isolated due to the introduction of additional variables, the learning opportunity for the experiment is lost. Project managers of innovation projects can help review experimental designs before they are executed and help ensure other experiments initiated elsewhere in the organization do not interfere with the learning process. Another area of failure is in the analysis of experimental results. Project managers can help facilitate analysis by ensuring properly trained individuals are performing the work and that the methodology used is current and consistent. Being active during the analysis of data can also provide the project manager with an understanding of the inter-relationships between experiments that may go unnoticed by only viewing individual results. In summary, there are three areas where a project manager can help improve the learning process of an innovation project:

1. **Rate-of-learning:** the speed at which a hypothesis can be converted into data and then analyzed to produce information

2. **Number of Learning-cycles:** the number of times a hypothesis can be converted into data and then analyzed to produce information within a given time period

3. **Quality of Learning:** the degree to which the information produced by an experiment is accurate and useful

Managing Project Risks

As discussed earlier in this book, project risk management is one of the most powerful levers a project manager has in ensuring project success. A first pass at a project risk-register should be available at the kickoff meeting before a project begins to be executed, however this is not a one time view of this critical document. Risk-registers should be reviewed and updated each time the project team meets, which should be at least weekly. The handling strategies defined for various risk statements should be converted into action items with discrete owners. Receiving a status on these action items at each team meeting is also part of the risk management process. Since there are always more risks to review than time available, the project manager must have a focused strategy to rooting out the most important discussions. The first order of business is to score any new risks that have been added to the register, followed by the development of a handling strategy for any red risks that have not yet been handled. Next, the team should review the previously defined handling strategies of the remaining red risk items, including any associated action items. For those handling strategies that have been implemented, the team should re-score that risk item to lower it within the risk-register ranking. Finally, the team should review the yellow-risks for any that directly affect the critical path of the project and then handle these as appropriate. While performing risk management on innovation projects, the project manager should always remain cognizant of the potential for innovations not to develop as anticipated and have contingency plans in place to keep the project on track. The key to this process working is the establishment of rough progress thresholds for critical work packages of the project plan. Given that innovations do not progress linearly, the project manager must establish the thresholds based on the environmental constraints of the innovation. For example, using the hypothetical scenario from earlier in this Chapter, if an engineer has three months to produce a solution and based on their environmental constraints, they are allotted nine lots to run experiments, the project manager should consider implementing a contingency plan if after six lots, the engineer still has not uncovered any positive correlations, indicating that the characterization of the process step is behind schedule. Obviously, this level of project management requires a highly sophisticated and proactive project manager that is capable of understanding the scientific methods supporting the process of innovation.

Managing Progressive Elaboration

The concept of progressive elaboration when applied to project management can be described as the improvement of a project plan over time, as more information is gained by the project team. Progressive elaboration is the concept that a project plan continuously improves over time by becoming more detailed, specific, and accurate. Each new iteration of the project plan builds on the prior plan and the experience and knowledge gained by the project team.

This improvement in project understanding should be captured by project managers as revisions to the project plan. In other words, the scope, schedule, and budget should always reflect the best information that is available at the time of their publication and should be re-published upon the acquisition of better information. This revision process of the project plan should not be confused with re-baselining a project, a common confusion among inexperienced project managers. A project plan should only be considered for re-baselining if one of the triple-constraints is going to change. Project revisions can occur without fundamentally changing the triple-constraint of the project. Another distinction is in the authority to change the project plan. Revisions to a project plan can be approved by the project manager, while re-baselined project plans must be approved by the project's sponsor, since they involve a new contract. One of the greatest mistakes made by project managers is agreeing to a change to the triple-constraint without re-baselining a project plan. For example, if a project sponsor suddenly informs a project manager that the project's budget needs to be reduced by 20% due to cost cutting measures, the inexperienced project manager will reluctantly agree to this change without increasing the duration or reducing the scope of the project. In other words, the project manager unwittingly agrees to continue with what has become an incongruent project. An experienced project manager will accept the 20% reduction in budget and then negotiate revisions to the scope and schedule to re-establish congruency. The experienced project manager knows there is no free lunch and will not continue managing a project that is destined for failure. The newly negotiated schedule, scope, and budget that re-establishes congruency with the 20% reduction in budget becomes the re-baselined project plan. Some project managers that agree to budget reductions without re-negotiating the triple-constraint feel they can be viewed as the hero if they still deliver the project on time and within scope. Unfortunately, when project managers choose this path, they often force the project team to work overtime to get the work done as scheduled. This additional work gets done for free, since most knowledge workers now fall under the employment category not eligible for overtime pay. From the project sponsor's perspective, the project was delivered according to the defined scope, within the allotted time, and with the 20% reduction in budget. This implies to the project sponsor that the project plan was padded, therefore setting up the expectation that future project can be cut by 20% will little effect to the overall plan. In reaction to this trend, project teams start to pad their estimates, which ultimately leads to deeper reductions in budget on future projects. An environment of mistrust spirals out of control until project management is no longer effective or value added to an organization and project teams are burned out from working excessive hours over long periods of time. To avoid this negative situation, a project manager has a responsibility to the company and the project team to force a re-negotiation of the triple-constraint, holding all progress on the project until congruency can be re-established.

Communication Pitfalls

During the implementation of a project, the project manager should follow the steps outlined in the communications plan and the specific communications tasks built into the schedule as discussed earlier in this book. Some of the information that should be communicated out to the stakeholder community includes progress status and performance-to-plan metrics. However, when reporting out on a project, it is important to avoid the six most common communication mistakes:

Failing to Identify the "Critical Few" Metrics

It's easy to measure everything that can be measured, but not very useful. There are typically only a handful of critical metrics that matter. For innovation projects, the best metrics are typically related to speed-of-learning and time-to-market. The higher up in the organization the person is who receives project performance information, the fewer indicators should be communicated. For example, if a CEO asks about a particular project, the best metric that can be provided is the payback period and return on investment. A lower level manager may benefit from metrics such as average full-time equivalents (FTE) per project, average time between phased-gate decision points, and so forth.

Measuring All Initiatives as if They Were Equal

Honest project managers do not hide problem areas within averages and summarized data. It's important to keep information at a level of granularity that allows the recipient to truly understand the health of a project. For example, if three experiments out of four are doing well, however the fourth is critical to the success of the project, do not roll up all the experiments under one banner that implies the project is on track. In other words, be sure to include relative magnitude when providing a project status.

Focusing Only Internally

Reporting on project performance-to-plan is important, however can be misleading if not also taking into consideration the changing environment. Project managers must focus on and report out on changes in market timing, customer demand, competitive landscapes, technological advances, cost structures, cost of capital, demographic shifts, and anything else that changes the fundamental assumptions of the project. It's important for the project manager to focus on climbing the project ladder efficiently, but not without also ensuring it is still leaning against the right building.

Measuring Activities Rather Than Results

Simply reporting out on resource consumption does not provide the recipient of the information any indication that the project is on track to meet its objectives. Project managers should instead focus on the number of scope features a project team has developed, or the number of objectives already met, or the overall percent of scope completed. This scoping related information is more valuable than the percent of schedule completed, or the percent of budget spent, which is often what gets reported.

Failing to Keep it Simple

When reporting processes add layers of bureaucracy to an organization, they have gone too far. Overly complex reports, or labor intensive metrics collection processes typically fail because people will simply not follow the process, or reports will be generated with fabricated information. The best reports are very simple to produce, focus on the critical few metrics, and can be quickly read and understood by the recipient. Large complex projects do not require large complex reports. The quality of the information should be the driver when communicating out on any project, large or small.

Using the Measurement System

Consistency in reporting is the key to maintaining project control. In many cases, just the practice of developing a status report forces the project team members to think through what has been accomplished and what can be done in the future to ensure success. Maintaining a regular reporting cycle, while not the most fun activity there is, can be analogous to maintaining a consistent exercise routine. Each report may not do much in terms of ensuring project success, however a consistent reporting process will help solidify the overall health of the project.

Chapter 8

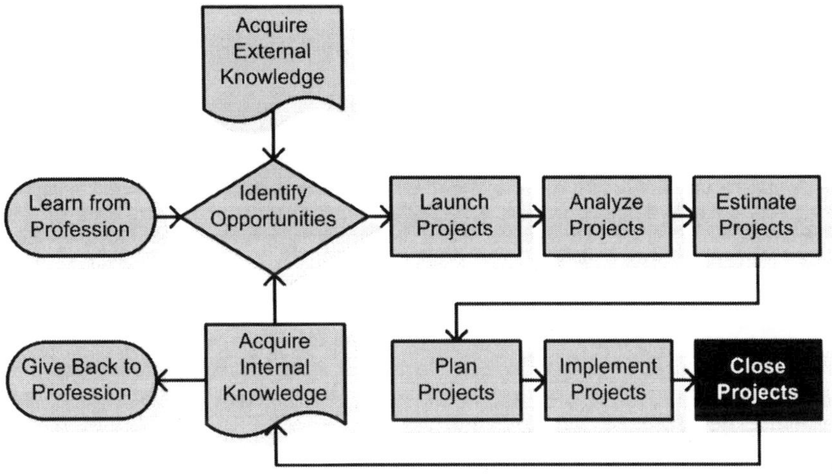

Concluding and Documenting

Projects are ready to conclude after the deliverables outlined in the scope document have been successfully delivered and the customer has accepted them as sufficiently meeting the objectives of the project. This acceptance triggers the project team to begin the project closure process. When innovation projects come to a close, in particular, there is typically a need to file for patents and document research in a knowledge management system. Project closure typically refers to all of the activities required to complete the project and disband the project team. Closure activities include the collection of project records, presentations, and analysis of the project's failures and successes. Lessons-learned should also be collected for input into the project's knowledge management system. Project teams can keep track of the step-by-step process of project closure by following a closeout and evaluation checklist and questionnaire.

Closeout Checklist

- ✓ Deliverables all completed and transferred to the sponsor/customer
- ✓ Project stakeholders notified of the closure of the project and provided with a final status on the results
- ✓ Project team members recognized for their contributions and future project assignments lined up
- ✓ Financial accounts reconciled and closed
- ✓ Results and lessons-learned captured in a knowledge management systems

Closeout Questions

1. Did the project solve the problem statement? If so, to what extent? What else could have been done?

2. If the problem was not completely solved by the project, why? What could have been done differently?
3. How well did the project follow the plan? Was the scope addressed completely? Was the schedule met? Was the budget met? If not, why?
4. Were deliverables early or late? Why? Did the customer receive the deliverables with full satisfaction? What, if anything, was missing?
5. How well did the project team perform? Was the right mix of skills and personalities assembled? What should change on the next project?
6. Did the project sponsor modify the schedule, scope, and/or budget during the execution of the project? Why was this done? What were the effects on the project? Was the project plan re-baselined with a congruent triple-constraint?
7. How can the next project be improved?

Innovation projects close just like all projects, although the measurements the project team will want to focus on in innovation projects are more related to the amount of learning achieved during the projects, the rate of that learning, as well as the number of learning-cycles achieved. Experimental designs should be reviewed for their overall effectiveness to determine if improvements in planning experiments can be realized. Data correlations should be documented and any new finding that may be leveraged across the enterprise should be highlighted and communicated. Other than delivering the results of the project, the main focus of the project team during the closure process should be to capture any intellectual property that was generated and make it available to the organization to further elaborate and commercialize. As will be discussed in Chapter 9, knowledge management systems are a great way to accomplish this task. Another best practice is the hosting of what NASA calls a "Masters Forum." These events are conducted after a project is complete and attended by the project's stakeholders, in addition to leaders across an the Agency involved with projects. By invitation only, Masters Forums are positioned as prestigious events where thought leaders gather to share ideas and further the collective body of knowledge. Industry experts are also invited to provide keynote addresses and serve as facilitators of break-out sessions. The agenda typically begins with a keynote address from a well respected industry leader on a topic related to the featured project. This address is then followed by a story of the project delivered by the project manager. He or she speaks to the audience in a very informal way, describing the personal interactions of the projects, the main decision points and how the team approached them, as well as the highs and lows of the project. It's the kind of discussion that you could imagine happening around a campfire, or in a cozy booth at your favorite restaurant. This storytelling session is followed by a panel discussion where the entire project team sits behind tables on a stage in front of the audience where a question and answer session is moderated by a professional facilitator. This section of the Masters Forum allows opportunity for the various stakeholders to gain clarification on the decision-making process and insight into what the project team would have done differently now that the project is complete. Many golden-nuggets are uncovered during this casual discussion. Next, the Masters Forum shifts focus from the featured project to the overall discipline of project management. To manage this part of the event, breakout sessions are organized around important topics of discussion, such as risk management, knowledge management, innovation projects, and the like. Finally, on the second day of the event, the entire audience is brought back together for several more discussions on lessons-learned and strategic changes for upcoming projects. The event comes to a close in the early afternoon, in time for participants to rest up for an evening dinner and social. Each phase of the Masters Forum offers opportunities for networking to transpire, ideas to be shared, and a common body of knowledge to be perpetuated and improved upon. It makes for a great way to wrap up a project and provides a mechanism for improving the organization in significant ways.

In many companies, project closure is often never completed, simply because inexperienced project teams are not sure what they should do and not clear on the purpose of the process. When viewed from a single project perspective, ignoring this closure step makes logical sense. However, when viewed from an enterprise perspective, this step in the management of projects is a critical components of continuous improvement.

Chapter 9

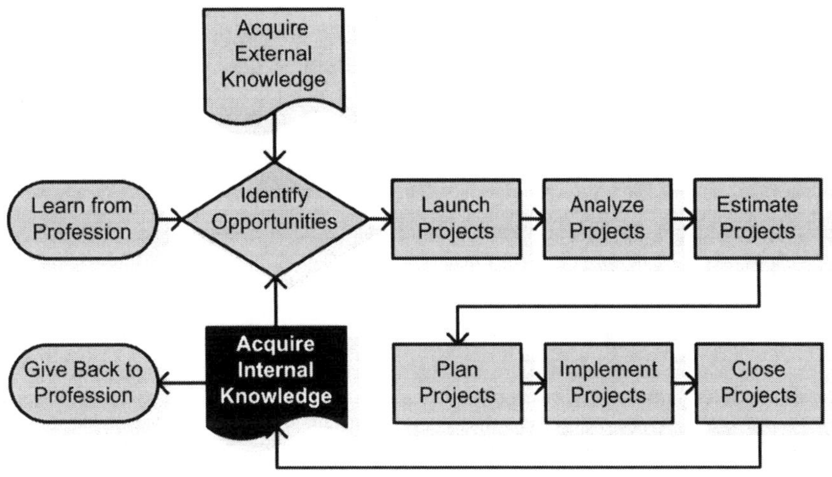

Managing Post-*Blue Sky* Project Knowledge

Once a project is complete, why spend the time collecting, organizing, and distributing information? From a single-project perspective, these activities make little difference to the outcome of the project. The value lies in the collective knowledge of the organization improving over time. With each completed project, the baseline organizational knowledge improves, thereby enabling better decision making. When planning for knowledge management, it's helpful to think of the corporation, or organization, as a physical entity, complete with its own brain function and neuro network. The brain, in this case, contains all the knowledge of the corporation, including best-practices, lessons-learned, special processes, patent ideas, and the like. The brain is manifested as a library of interconnected databases, much like what we know today as the Internet. Using this design, each node in the network represents a distinct body of knowledge. The nervous system in this analogy is made up of various communication channels using a combination of push and pull distribution techniques. Points of knowledge access, such as mobile devices and computer terminals are akin to neural receptors. Just like in a physical body where brain signals provide information to body parts that in turn react in informed ways, a great knowledge management system can distribute knowledge at just the right time to a company's knowledge workers, who in turn make more informed decisions.

The keys to making knowledge management systems effective are to ensure that unnecessary data is filtered out, important data is synthesized into actionable information, and intelligence is built into the input and output functions of the interface. NASA is an organization that has led the world in knowledge management research. They have spent many years and millions of dollars to develop what is known today as the NEN, or NASA Engineering Network. This knowledge management system is sponsored by the Office of the Chief Engineer and focuses on distributing lessons-learned from its many programs to each of the nine NASA Centers and the Jet Propulsion Laboratory. Their public website reveals,

The NASA Engineering Network was created as a knowledge network to promote learning and sharing among NASA's engineers. Through engineering communities of practice, NASA Lessons-learned, agency-wide search, expertise locator, and training, NASA's engineers are connected to engineering resources that help them effectively and efficiently solve problems and design solutions.

I was working with NASA during the introduction of the NEN, which was made possible after a series of restructurings across the Agency. Often what keeps these initiatives from succeeding is politics played out between the various knowledge domain owners. Only until organizations are willing to share information, which represents power, without immediate reciprocation, will these initiatives have a chance.

Knowledge management systems must be designed in such a way that information assimilation becomes natural for the knowledge worker. However, the most important part of a knowledge management system, which can propel a company forward in efficiency and effectiveness, is its content. Content is king, you may have heard, and this phrase holds true when speaking of knowledge management systems. Content can be discussed according to its characteristics, including quality and depth. One often overlooked characteristic of content, which is critical to innovation organizations, is breadth. For innovation companies in particular, there are twenty main focus areas in which content should be developed and made available through a knowledge management system.

Portfolio Consistency

Corporate strategic planning typically takes place annually in earnest, with six month refreshes of the plan. From this activity, a set of corporate themes, focus areas, and objectives emerge. This information is critical to project teams seeking to align their projects with what is important to the business. The information also serves as input to project evaluation matrices, which ensure all projects are selected and funded according to the same criteria. By simply posting a company's strategy and objectives in a central repository, team members can have access to the information they need to march in the same direction. Many executives are surprised when they learn that employees below their immediate direct reports often do not know what the corporate strategy is; or if they do they are confused by it. Tech-savvy companies supplement their corporate plans with video interviews of the CEO explaining the rationale of the plan in terms that everyone can understand. Also critical to this alignment is the development and communication of supporting strategic plans by each of the organizations. The larger the company, the more important it is to have a portfolio of strategic plans to help focus the workforce. Without these plans, employees feel disconnected from the top of the company and are not sure how their function contributes to the high-level objectives.

Evaluating Opportunities

Marketing research plays a big part in the innovation process by identifying market trends, competitive positions, and gaps of unmet opportunity. Marketing serves a great role in every organization, however their information is often only made available to the executive team. Because of this tight relationship, marketing organizations begin to work in a vacuum, cut off from the operations. The value of market related information is not leveraged across the broader organization unless is can be made available in a manner that is actionable to decision makers. Another aspect of this content area that adds tremendous value to decision making is the identification of changes in company direction as a result of market shifts. Reading about market changes in the media is entirely too late to gain advantage over your competition. Investing in marketing research experts pays dividends to many companies, as this information forms the tip of the arrow of decision making.

Prioritizing Growth Initiatives

Knowing the priority of key innovations required to drive corporate growth is necessary to sequence experiments and projects. Many research organizations accomplish this through the development of technology roadmaps that visually establish the timing and priority of emerging technologies. Establishing an overall critical path for innovation enables managers to focus on those activities that will enable additional downstream activities. Communicating priorities across an organization using a knowledge management system will aid in gaining buy-in for smaller, unknown technology projects that would not normally show up on anyone's radar screen. Organizing and communicating priorities in this manner can introduce a level of agility in decision making that many large companies have lost.

Consolidating Enterprise Projects

One of the biggest wastes of time and money among innovation companies is the duplication of effort. In most cases, this duplication is not intentional, it is simply caused by ignorance of the other activities underway in the organization. By identifying all the key initiatives planned and in progress across an organization, the ability of project teams to work together and consolidate activities is thereby enabled. Consolidation of projects is a great way to reduce overall costs and minimize confusion among the workforce. When evaluating consolidation opportunities, the review must be conducted both within functional organizations and across the organizations. In other words, an enterprise scan must be preformed with the entire process becoming transparent through a knowledge management system.

Demonstrating Project Pipeline Returns

Knowing the ROI of a company's innovation project pipeline is important to predict future earnings and plan downstream capital expenditures. It also serves as a gage to company executives as to whether they have a large enough pipeline based on historical failure rates. The pipeline is a great analogy to the process that innovation projects follow at a macro level. Ideas enter the large end of a tapered pipe with dollars exiting the smaller end. The taper of the pipe represents the failure rate of ideas converting into profits, while the length of the pipe represents the average time it takes to convert. Communicating this information across the company gives project sponsors a traffic-light indicator as to when they need to fund new projects. Also communicating metrics around the conversion rate and speed of conversion is an effective way to drive the right behaviors and decisions.

Project Management Discipline

Pipeline productivity requires the concerted enforcement of the discipline of project management. This enforcement, often referred to as project management governance, can be deployed via a project management office, which can become a bureaucratic burden on an organization; or by the effective use of a knowledge management system, the preferable approach. Project management methodologies, as well as supporting templates, can be communicated, and made available, through an online project management portal. The test is to audit a cross-section of key projects underway across an organization by reviewing the various processes and templates with the goal of spotting divergence. Through education and effective deployment of knowledge management systems, companies can reduce the "reinvention of the wheel" syndrome experienced by many less proactive organizations. The ultimate goal in this endeavor is to create a projectized culture where following good project management methodologies becomes, "just the way we do business." Lao Tzu, the ancient Chinese philosopher, said it best when he described the various levels of good governance roughly 3,000 years ago,

> *When the master governs, the people are hardly aware that he exists. Next best is a leader who is loved. Next, one who is feared. The worst is one who is despised. If you don't trust the people, you make them untrustworthy. The Master doesn't talk, he acts. When his work is done, the people say, "Amazing: we did it, all by ourselves!"*

Optimizing Cross-Functional Resources

In many companies, employees are assigned solely to functional groups, causing the approval process to participate on cross-functional projects difficult to navigate. If participation is allowed, the percent of available time allocated toward cross-functional tasks is typically low, with priority given to primary job responsibilities. Traditional organizational structures often result in project teams comprised of overworked members with their attention split among many higher priority tasks. To further demoralize team members, incentives are tied to primary job responsibilities, rather than project success rates. A better way to help projects succeed is to designate full-time project managers, leaders, and subject-matter experts. These resources should be completely allocated to projects and preferably reporting into a program manager, or equivalent position. Using this organizational design, a portfolio of project talent can be organized and communicated across and enterprise. The expertise of the resources, as well as their availability to take on new projects, can be made available cross-functionally using a knowledge management system. As new strategic projects are approved, project sponsors can help pull together the optimal project team from across the organization, thereby increasing the probability of project success and rewarding employees for performance. This system can also work in reverse; as projects come to a close, employees can review upcoming projects and then request that they be considered for inclusion on the project team. This natural selection process will ensure that the best workers are working on the most exciting and innovative projects.

Facilitating Technology Transfer

Pure research often goes unnoticed by the larger organization because it is not communicated broadly enough that the technology is available for commercialization. Many companies spend millions of dollars developing huge patent portfolios only to later watch them expire without ever making a dime off of the investment. A properly designed and deployed knowledge management system can increase the probability that investments in innovation will bear fruit, as well as the odds that new interrelated ideas will emerge by the mere juxtaposition of various patents displayed in a portfolio. Fundamentally, the best way to transfer technologies from incubation to commercialization is by communicating their value propositions in such ways that non-technical "MBA" types can understand their downstream application and develop a business plan for their use.

Demonstrating Prototype Viability

Integration partners and industrial customers usually like to "see" what a technology looks like in application before committing to investments in tooling, inventory, and other capital expenditures. Speaking about the potential of an innovation is not enough to convince cash strapped investors to open their checkbooks. Innovation companies must have channels to communicate marketable technologies with enough detail that prospects are convinced of the viability of the product. Knowledge management systems can port real project data that is filtered for customer consumption, thereby reducing the overhead burden of information duplication. Also, information configuration is no longer an issue, since reports that the project teams use and the customers review are supplied by the same databases. Prototype demonstration becomes even more integrated when dealing with digital models of physical parts. Manufacturing instructions, material properties, and engineering analysis can be embedded within a computer developed model that can be modified by engineers and viewed by customers simultaneously. Alibre Inc., for example, has become a leading software provider in this market by enabling engineers and customers across the globe to collaborate on part design, development, and manufacturing.

Promoting Platform Efficiency

Innovation is only successful if it can produce a profit for the company that made the initial investment. To help ensure profitability, engineers must stay focused on cost reduction opportunities during the development. This is made possible by using standardized modules of technology that combine with the innovation to make a new product. Unfortunately, these cost reduction opportunities are often missed due to lack of awareness of the existing technologies. Engineers spend unproductive time re-developing technology that should be as simple as plug and play. Knowledge management can alleviate this issue by communicating company approved standard technologies available for development of new products. This concept is already heavily used in the auto industry, for example, but has not yet become standard practice in high-tech. As foreign competition continues to drive down margins in high-tech, innovation reuse will become a topic of much discussion.

Monitoring External Technologies

Competitive intelligence helps keep companies on the same playing field, however most automated data supplied through these channels is sales focused in nature, not covering technology trends. Regarding technical innovations across an industry, the common, albeit manual, way of gathering this critical information is through trade shows, conferences, symposiums, and seminars. In fact, most companies spend quite a bit of time and money sending engineers to these events to gather information that may aid in future decision making and benchmarking. Unfortunately, once engineers return from these trips, they get absorbed back into the daily grind with little time to document and share what they have learned. Knowledge management systems can help solve this issue by providing easy to navigate text entry fields where engineers can quickly provide the salient points from a trip, including relevant URL links to additional data. With just a little data entry, important information can be disseminated across an organization, thereby turning an expensive travel assignment into an investment that will pay dividends far into the future.

Attracting Innovation Partners

Providing a compelling value proposition to a potential partner in innovation requires the ability to share important primary research and other critical data that the partner would not otherwise have access to in the marketplace. Knowledge management systems can facilitate this transaction by providing user-specific access to patent portfolio data, test results, whitepapers, and the like, via secure logins. Companies can control what data a partner has access to and ensure proprietary data is not accessible. Furthermore, they can segment their knowledge database by partner, allowing research funded by one partner to remain confidential and inaccessible by another partner. Knowledge management systems can also be networked with the knowledge management systems of consortia, to eliminate the need for double entry of data.

Promoting Collaborative Development

Collaboration with partners sharing risk on a development is critical to program success. One of the primary issues in these arrangements is often the inability to link two or more companies together to promote effective communication. Different network firewalls, system configurations, and geographic distances between the partners makes the challenge even more daunting. Fortunately, web enabled knowledge management systems can bridge the gaps between partners by providing a robust repository to store and disseminate program data. Furthermore, collaboration tools can be launched and operated from a single knowledge management system, allowing greater control over application licensing arrangements.

Managing University Relationships

University research programs are typically initiated to produce primary research, however in competitive environments the value decay of this information is rapid. It's critical to get the research into the minds of development engineers as it becomes available. Waiting until formal papers are compiled and published could cause a company to miss a narrow window of opportunity. By utilizing a knowledge management system as a repository for experimental data, most promising hypothesis, and key findings and correlations, development engineers can get early perspectives on technologies that are not yet fully baked, but nevertheless very valuable to future products and services.

Managing Innovation Partnerships

Processes for evaluating partnerships must be developed and managed to ensure the time and energy investment has a positive ROI. To facilitate the evaluation, metrics should be established and populated by real-time data within a knowledge management system. Using the system in this way enables drill-down functionality into underlying technical specifications that combine to produce a particular innovation. With access to this type of data, partners can quickly evaluate the level of participation on innovation projects, as well as their contributions toward the innovation in terms of patentable ideas.

Sharing Technical Knowledge

Sharing knowledge is the primary purpose of any knowledge management system, with an overall objective of enabling more effective decision making. Once a knowledge management system is in place in an organization, the metric to gage the value revolves around decision quality. This is a difficult metric to capture and measure, but one worth the effort. One way research companies tackle this task is by evaluating the results of experiments against their intended outcome. Over time, the gap between what an experiment was supposed to correlate versus what it did correlate should decrease in size as knowledge management systems increase in information and usage.

Mapping Workforce Supply and Demand

Analyzing resource and skill supply requires human resource data to be available across an enterprise. Through the use of knowledge management systems, employers can capture profiles of their most valuable assets, their employees. Imagine the performance improvements that a business can achieve when it maps skills with projects to ensure the best fit. Companies can also forecast skill shortages and gap, thereby focusing its recruiting efforts in strategic ways, rather than on filling every vacant position. Mergers and acquisitions can be used to fill major talent gaps, but only if this information is collected and made available.

Analyzing Workforce Career Preferences

Using the same employee profiles mentioned above, companies can utilize this platform to gain an understanding of their professional expectations in training, responsibility, and advancement. By proactively preparing employees for the next challenge, companies will benefit by greater loyalty and a more motivated workforce. More and more companies are nothing more than collections of knowledge workers providing services for clients. Disregarding the needs of this collective asset is like never servicing your only means of transformation. Before long the engine will blow and you will be left stranded. Companies must be good stewards of their assets by ensuring that their employees feel they are self-actualizing in their careers.

Leveraging Skills Across the Enterprise

Could you imagine just-in-time staffing from an internal workforce? This approach to applying resources to projects would revolutionize the business world by introducing a level of efficiency only seen in start-up operations. Redundant positions, which now are common place, would be greatly reduced, as would the need for many layers of management. Project managers could tap into internal subject-matter experts much like they would hire a consultant, although under this scenario the advertisement would be a knowledge management system organized much like the popular professional networking site www.linkedin.com.

Structuring Effective Teams

One of the most effective ways of improving the success rate of projects is to pay project team members for performance. To accomplish this task objectively, companies must establish team based goals with clearly defined success criteria. Using the SMART method of goal creation is recommended. SMART refers to Specific, Measurable, Attainable, Relevant, and Timely. Incentive pay plans can use several methods of payouts, including interpolation, pass/fail, and target based. Interpolation means that a range of goal results are defined from least favorable to most. Then the payout becomes a percentage along that range, where 100% is achieve for a most favorable result. Pass/fail payouts are straight forward; you either achieve the results and get a 100% payout, or you don't. Target based payouts typically involve three acceptable goal results ranging from least favorable to most. The least favorable is paid out at 50% of the agreed upon payment. The middle target is set at a level where the results are highly beneficial and deserve a 100% payout. The third target should be considered a stretch to achieve with a lower probability of reaching. These targets are typically paid out at 125% of the established dollar amount. Whichever payout method your company chooses, the point is that people respond to performance based incentive plans and these programs can be facilitated using well designed knowledge management systems.

The Value of Storytelling

Much can be debated around the purpose and design of knowledge management systems. Knowledge management is certainly one of the most important business topics of this generation, but also one of the most misunderstood. When discussing knowledge management, the conversation typically migrates to a technical debate of the use of software and the tagging of discrete data for later access. Though these aspects are important, they are secondary to the primary essence of a knowledge management system, which is how information will be presented to a knowledge worker. Our first inclination is to work on the format of a standard report to make it easier to navigate, or develop executive dashboards with high-level indicators supported by drill-down access to underlying data. However important these communication vehicles are, they still pale in comparison to the natural method by which all humans learn – listening to stories. Since the dawn of civilization, mankind has passed on valuable information through storytelling. Some of these stories were also converted to cave paintings and sculptures, yet they were still stories. What is it about this simple methodology that makes it so effective in transferring important information? To answer this question we must understand the concepts of cognitive psychology. When we receive information, our brains do not store it alphabetically in a mental file cabinet. In fact, there is no such thing as a file cabinet structure in our brains. Our brains are more like the web of the Internet. Information nodes are connected to one another by a multitude of links that form a three-dimensional network capable of retrieving data from multiple nodes using parallel processing. Unfortunately, we also have access limitations similar to that of an electrical signal passed through a long cable - distance causes the signal to weaken. To overcome this natural law, our brains use some memory nodes as signal boosters, or amplifiers. So, what does all this have to do with storytelling, you might ask? When we hear stories and apply the concepts to our own experiences, many of our memory nodes are activated – much more than would be activated by reading a report. As these memory nodes become active, they become ready to add new links to new nodes of information. In other words, the memory network in our brain that becomes active while hearing a story serves as the context, or canvas for the new concepts. Fortunately, this canvas is not blank, in fact it is covered with an elaborate work of art known as your understanding. Like a master artist, your brain adds to this work of art, or understanding, as it becomes exposed to new information. This is a natural process that provides us with the incredible ability to recall a complex concept by simply smelling a familiar fragrance, or seeing a familiar color. Great communicators know how to leverage this cognitive process when motivating and rallying the troops around a common message.

Jack Welch is a believer in using stories to motivate workers. When he was busy turning around GE in the 1980s, he often repeated a conversation he had with the managers of the nuclear-engineering group after the Three Mile Island meltdown occurred. These managers presented their business plan still assuming that they would continue to sell nuclear-power plants into the United States. After listening to their plan, he responded with a pointed statement that they would very likely never sell another nuclear-power plant. He urged them to go back and develop a plan that didn't involve selling more reactors. They went back to the drawing board and came up with a compelling plan to offer services to existing customers. When Jack told this story to other groups across GE, it forced them to question their own paradigms about their markets and their future prospects. This story served as a great way to get people to think deeply and internally.

Chapter 10

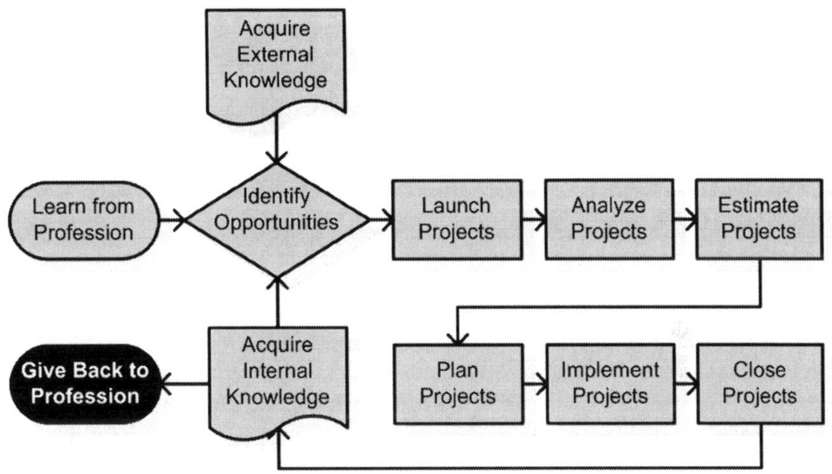

The Profession of Project Management

It's amazing how many MBA students keep their hands lowered when asked if they are currently project managers. After a little prompting and a story about the project of making a sandwich, all students typically raise their hand admitting they are, in fact, project managers. The point gets across quickly that we should all seek to be the best managers of projects that we can be, whether we are homemakers, MBA students, or corporate executives.

The need for skilled project managers is beginning to get the attention of corporate executives eager to grow their businesses.

Top executives are reporting that project management is a key part of their growth strategies. Project management is starting to be viewed as an important lever in improving performance overall. One of its most compelling characteristics it that the discipline of project management can be utilized across all industries and in all countries – it is truly a world-class business methodology. Research concludes, the pressure to deliver projects on time and on budget puts project management skills atop the list of hiring priorities for a majority of executives. A majority have plans to train their staff in project management and about one third have plans to hire project managers in the near future. Fortunate for project managers, their numbers are in short supply.

The demand for project management talent is growing both in the United States and abroad, as more work is moved to emerging countries. Companies need people who can manage many moving parts within diverse cultures. Trained project managers are typically the perfect blend of technically competent leader, business savvy liaison, and effective communicator, which makes them ideal for global positions. Offshoring has also spawned many new opportunities for global project management. For those willing, interested, and able to work in foreign countries, such as India and Russia, the opportunities could be tremendous. Other reports indicate that project management is the skill-set that is most associated with job advancement and considered the best discipline to get ahead in the work place.

The demand for project management is really just beginning in the United States as Federal agencies are in the process of bolstering their ranks of trained project managers in response to a directive from the Office of Management and Budget. In 2005, the Bush administration launched an effort to improve the way information technology projects are managed across government. The initiative aims to train IT workers to become more competent project managers. The ramifications of this directive are considerable, given that these same Federal agencies are beginning to require their contractors to provide certified project managers, a requirement written into the statements of work. The list of Fortune 500 companies that earn a portion of their revenues from Federal contracts is quite extensive, therefore the demand generated by these companies for project management talent is on the verge of increasing exponentially. Combine this with the workforce population decline in the U.S. attributed to the baby-boomer retirement trend, and you can imagine the human-capital crisis that is soon to explode. U.S. citizens with project management certification, in particular, will be increasingly sought after, hitting an inflection point of demand in the year 2010, with a major gap developing by 2020. Figure 10.1 depicts the relationships between these trends.

DEMOGRAPHIC CURVE

FIGURE 10.1

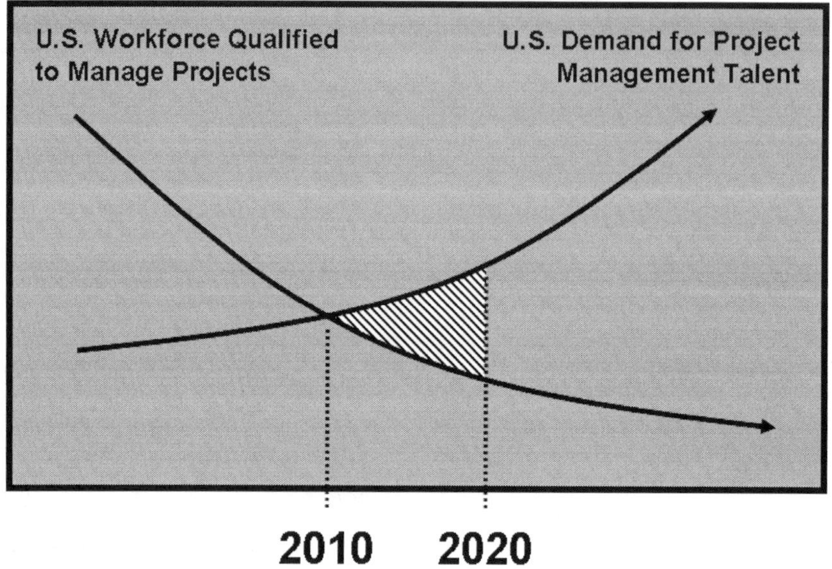

There is ample evidence to indicate that project management skills are in demand and will be in the foreseeable future, however the tasks which a project manager must perform are not all fun and games.

The Role of a Project Manager

Project Management is considered a technical position, although many non-technical people excel in the role. The position requires a tremendous amount of communication (some estimate 80%) to be effective; an area where right brained creative types perform best. Also important are the abilities to negotiate and sell. Project managers are constantly reinforcing the importance of their projects to weary stakeholders and tired team members, as well as negotiating the tradeoffs between the triple-constraints of schedule, scope, and budget. Project management is often the sole responsibility of a project manager. They are directly involved with the activities to produce an end product, service, or result, however do not typically participate in the final outcome. Project managers are not wired for marathon operations activities, but rather trained to sprint to the finish line with a successful result. Project managers work with clients to develop requirements, they then synthesize these requirements into plans that will orchestrate teams of people to bring the concepts to reality. A successful project manager must be able to envision the entire project from start to end and have the ability to ensure the vision comes to fruition.

This definition captures the essence of what a project manager does, which is quite vague as you may have noticed. Project management is much like general management where the business unit is constantly changing; it is a highly dynamic field to be sure. Sometimes it's helpful to define project management by what it is not, which is operations. The definition of a project helps shape the boundaries of the position. A project is referred to as a temporary set of activities undertaken to create a unique product, service, or result. By definition, people involved in activities that have no end, or are producing repeatable outcomes, are not involved in project management. People interested in new challenges and constant change would be well advised to research the position of project manager, however not everyone is predisposed for this line of work.

Personality of a Project Manager

It has been said that the ideal project manager would have doctorate degrees in engineering, business, and psychology, with experience in at least ten different companies scattered across a variety of diverse industries. They would also have the energy of a twenty-five year old combined with the judgment of a seasoned executive and have the ability to speak multiple languages. Obviously this person doesn't exists, although many hiring managers think they do, based on a majority of the position descriptions posted on the Internet. While it may be impossible to fit the ideal, we can understand our personal characteristics better and focus on accentuating those. One great way to get to the heart of who we are is to complete a personality assessment. These tests can be administered at your local university, or online for a fee at a variety of sites. There are also a few free online sources if you hunt for them. Most tests will provide a four letter code that correlates with a personality type. There are sixteen possible combinations of personality types with four main project management related categories: visionary, analyst, facilitator, and historian.

The Visionary (5% of the population)

Visionary types can envision the future and use projects to accomplish larger objectives in an organization. They often work well as program managers and can easily spot all the interdependencies among a portfolio of complex projects. They are often opinionated, assertive, and highly imaginative. Visionaries are on the continual hunt for new opportunities and process improvements. Visionaries embrace continuous improvement initiatives since they allow the creation of new ways to accomplish work. They are comfortable leading projects and prefer to be in that position. Visionaries are often charismatic and can inspire people to participate in their projects. They can network well and sell projects to a wide variety of stakeholders. Visionaries are also comfortable navigating political waters and can exercise good judgment to get work done. Visionaries work well with ambiguity and prefer not to get bogged down in the details. They often delegate detail intensive tasks to other team members. Their project power comes from their ability to inspire and motivate others, as well as their tremendous communications skills.

The Analyst (20% of the population)

Analysts are focused on the details of getting the work done. They gravitate toward action and hard work, while ensuring other team members are driven by the project's objectives. They stay on task throughout the project lifecycle and do not waver from the project plan. Analysts are great planners and very self-disciplined. They gain their power from their knowledge of facts and details.

The Facilitator (20% of the population)

Facilitators are great at bringing together cross-functional teams to collaborate on certain aspects of a project. They often serve as project ambassadors by representing the interests of the project among interested stakeholder groups. Facilitators can also smooth over tense moments among project team members by addressing the perspectives and concerns of varying personalities. Facilitators hold relationships in high regard and work toward establishing mutual respect among peers. They gain their power from an ability to facilitate compromises among diverse opinions.

The Historian (55% of the population)

Historians recognize the need for documentation and work toward bringing order to chaos through policy and guidelines. They are good at rooting out data and supplying criteria for decision making. Historians can be thought of as puzzle-solvers, seeking out all the pieces to a project, then assembling them to reveal the end result. They are precise and consistent in their communications. Their power is derived from their ability to apply logic and structure to a project.

Personality Test Results

The results from personality tests can be used to select the right mix of personalities for a project team. The data suggests that 40-45% of the population is suitable for the position of project manager.

The Visionary Group:

INTJ – 100% Project Manager Aptitude

INTP – 50% Project Manager Apptitude/50% Team Member

INFJ – 100% Team Member Aptitude

INFP – 100% Unsuited for Project Management

The Analyst Group:

ENTJ – 100% Project Manager Aptitude

ENTP – 50% Project Manager Apptitude/50% Team Member

ENFJ – 50% Project Manager Apptitude/50% Team Member

ENFP – 50% Team Member Apptitude/50% Unsuited

The Facilitator Group:

ISTJ – 100% Project Manager Aptitude

ISFJ – 100% Team Member Aptitude

ISFP – 100% Unsuited

ISTP – 100% Unsuited

The Historian Group:

ESTJ – 100% Project Manager Aptitude

ESFJ – 50% Project Manager Apptitude/50% Team Member

ESTP – 50% Project Manager Apptitude/50% Unsuited

ESFP – 100% Unsuited

Project Management Training and Certification

There are numerous training opportunities available today for project management, so many in fact that choosing which route to take can be quite daunting. Fortunately, however, they all boil down into three main categories: university degree programs, university certification programs, and Project Management Professional (PMP) certification preparation programs. Selecting which of the three categories to pursue depends largely on your career aspirations. Let's review each option in greater detail.

University Degree Programs

This relatively new option has been driven by the overwhelming corporate demand for managers trained in project management. Many of the world's most reputable universities are now offering specialized masters degrees in project management. These are much like traditional business degrees with a heavy emphasis on general management and operations. This option is ideal for students who wish to obtain a masters degree in business and would like to focus on project management in the core classes. Traditional business degrees typically have only a single class devoted to project management, where specialized degree programs often have five or more project management related classes. The George Washington University (GWU) is one of the front runners in project management education. In 1996, GWU began planning a Graduate Project Management Program in the Department of Management Science of the School of Business offering a Master of Science Degree. This initiative reflected the University's eagerness to assess contemporary demands in government and industry and to incorporate new solutions into a progressive curriculum. Now the program presents an innovative curriculum that focuses on achieving a balance of practice and theory in project management. The curriculum was carefully compiled and is continually improved to include the skills that project managers need and other professionals wish to acquire when making the transition from team members to project managers. Another leading university offering focused programs in project management is the Stevens Institute of Technology in Hoboken, New Jersey. Stevens offers a Masters of Science in Management with a concentration in Project Management. They work closely with many government agencies wishing to integrate systems engineering and project management.

Most university degree programs are accredited by the Project Management Institute (PMI), which is a must have. In fact, Stevens was the third university worldwide to receive PMI accreditation. Many universities today also offer online versions of their degree programs, such at the Masters of Science in Management degree with a specialization in Project Management offered by Boston University online.

It would be impossible to list all the available university options in this book. One of the best resources for up to date information on degree programs in project management can be found at www.usnews.com. The next category for consideration is also offered primarily by universities, but is designed for students who would like to supplement an existing university degree, or are seeking a strong foundation in project management without wanting to spend the additional time and money required for a degree program.

University Certification Programs

Also accredited by PMI, university certification programs are a great way to learn the formal approach to project management. Many students come to these types of program having worked on project teams, or having served as a project manager for many years. They are good at their jobs, but are missing the understanding of the methodology and how all the elements work together. In addition to knowledge, students also seek the credibility a certification can provide in their current places of work, as well as in the job market. These programs also offer a great foundation in the discipline of project management prior to preparing for the PMP exam. Project management information is much broader than what a single course can cover, which is why these certification programs are so valuable. They typically cover the subject in a series of focused classes, such as the six course project management certification offered by the University of Phoenix (UoP). UoP programs are available online, on campus in Phoenix, Arizona, as well as via Flexnet, which is a combination of online and instructor-led classes held at local campuses across the United States. A UoP Flexnet project management certification program recently kicked off in November 2007 in Boise, Idaho. It is currently drawing students from nearby Micron Technology, Hewlett Packard, as well as a cross-section of small businesses in the area. For information on programs in your area visit their site at www.phoenix.edu. Once a student has completed either their university degree in project management, or certification in project management, it is recommended that they prepare for the PMP exam administered by PMI.

PMP Certification Preparation Programs

Preparing for the PMP exam has grown into a significant market over the years, attracting a large number of providers of preparation classes. Many of these providers will guarantee the passing of the exam or your money back, although it is not recommended that you choose a provider solely on this basis. A simple Google search on "PMP prep" reveals about 140,000 hits, consisting of a combination of books, instructor-led classes, and online tutorials. The method that you choose should depend on your style of learning. Most people learn best in instructor-led classes. Some of the most popular instructor-led training providers include Cheetah Learning, boasting a 97% pass rate in 2006 and quoting a $10,000 pay increase for PMP certification holders on average. Another popular provider is RMC Project Management founded by Rita Mulcahy in 1991. Most of these providers now offer books, instructor-led classes, and online training, which enables the bundling of all three for a lower price than if purchased individually. One approach that worked well for me was the use of online practice exams. Again, there are many providers of this service. PMCampus.com is one provider that offers 100% online training in an easy to use interface, as well as the posting of your 35 PDU credits with PMI upon completion of the practice exams - a requirement to sit for the PMP exam. Simply purchasing a book and running through practice exams seems like a logical approach, however some students find the transition to the computer based testing environment to be difficult. Completing the practice exams online is the ideal method, as most providers attempt to simulate the environment that will be available for the real exam – a huge benefit. Using online providers also ensures the latest wording of the exam questions are available. Many printed books are obsolete by the time they are published. Once you have made the commitment to obtain your PMP, plan on spending about three months studying for one hour each day, or about 90 hours in total. Crash courses are also available, but typically require about 40 hours of dedicated study over a five day period. PMI also offers other credentials, such as the CAPM for less experienced project managers and a new certification in program management. As both of these certifications are relatively new, as compared with the PMP, their global awareness is low, therefore their market value is still quite low. The PMP credential is the one worth the investment of time and money.

Advancing the Profession of Project Management

We all know that giving back is important, but often plan to wait until retirement before getting started. Given the fact that most of the people reading this book will never officially retire anyway, make a plan today to help advance the profession of project management.

In 1881, The Wharton School of the University of Pennsylvania launched the first business school in the world. Harvard followed in 1910 with the first MBA. Within 100 years of the first business school, business degrees grew to become one of the hottest courses of study and a recognized management science. This rapid ascent of management science did not occur without the support of people sold on the value. Similar to the study of business, the same demand has been building for the study of project management. To focus this demand and serve as a governing body, the Project Management Institute formed in 1969. Project ahead 100 years to 2108 and try to imagine what will be happening in the field of project management. Will all companies be projectized? Will the concept of an employee be replaced with independent project experts that form temporary global ventures to accomplish results? Will the position of Chief Project Officer (CPO) be commonplace? Will our children earn Ph.D. degrees in project management? Will universities devote large portions of their endowment toward the research of project management?

The possibilities are enormous, but will require a concerted effort from each of us to realize the potential of project management. To help in this mission, we can take the initiative of teaching project management in local universities, our places of work, or PMI Chapters. Speaking in primary schools about the career of a project manager is another way to generate interest in the study of project management. Consider serving on the board of a local PMI Chapter, helping it grow its membership or building awareness within the business community in your area. Educating employers on the value of project management is also a great way to open up the corporate purse string to fund the interests of project management. It's also possible to contribute to the advancement of project management by performing primary research, writing whitepapers, and speaking at symposiums. These are only a handful of examples to consider. There are many more options available, obviously. The point is to pick a way to advance the cause of project management that feels comfortable to you and then just do it! Together we can help shape the future of project management.

Continuous Improvement

Continuous improvement as applied to project management involves re-tooling methodologies to match the changing demands of the project environment, reading the latest research on managing innovation projects, defining terminology, adding to a taxonomy, refining templates, and re-thinking paradigms. Taking time to reflect on our inefficiencies and making plans to improve our performance after each project is an effective way to ensure we are continually adding value to our teams and improving our marketability as world-class project managers.

Appendix

Blue Sky Performance Metrics

- Percent of revenue/profit attributed to new products/services released in the past n-years
- Percent of revenue/profit attributed to new patents issues in the past n-years
- Return on investment in research and development (R&D)
- Percent of revenue/profit attributed to technology licensing and/or royalty income
- Percent of revenue/profit attributed to subscriptions/recurring income
- Degree of customer satisfaction with new products/services within first 90/180/360 days of purchase
- New product/service commercialization/failure rate
- Cadence between successive product launches
- Time-to-innovation (learning-cycle time)
- Time-to-market (development cycle time)
- Time-to-profit (break-even time)
- Average revenue/profit per full-time equivalent (FTE)
- Average number of experiments run per new product/service

- Average number of prototypes/mock-ups built per product/service
- Average percentage reuse of key platform elements
- Number of products/projects in active development
- Number of ideas/concepts screened/reviewed
- Percentage of ideas/concepts accepted/rejected
- Percentage of defined products/projects accepted/rejected
- Number of active products/projects per FTE
- Number of Learning-cycles per product/service
- Average duration of learning-cycles per product/service
- Percent of total FTE working in Front-Room/Back-Room
- Net Present Value (NPV) of product portfolio /pipeline /concepts
- Percent of product portfolio in long-cycle/short-cycle markets
- Percent of R&D FTE versus total/trend
- Total patents filed/pending/awarded per FTE/year
- Total licenses granted and/or acquired per FTE/year
- Number of disruptive technologies created per FTE/year
- R&D budget as a percentage of revenue
- Average development cost per project/product/service
- Average capital cost per project/product/service
- Average cash expense cost per project/product/service
- Extent of product/service differentiation

About the Author

John R. Maculley, Jr., MBA, PMP

Mr. Maculley spent nearly two decades helping a diverse group of start-up technology businesses, Fortune 500 corporations, and U.S. government agencies execute on their strategies and improve their operations. Most of his consulting assignments have been in the aerospace and high tech industries, with brief stints in software. He also teaches business classes at the university level to stay connected with the most current management concepts before they are published. Mr. Maculley looks for challenging engagements where the client's prior efforts have typically failed - the kind of projects where change can produce exponential growth. Some of his current and prior projects include the following:

Small Business

- Iventa [interim chief operating officer/off-shoring/customer relationship management]
- Digital Gateway [interim chief operating officer and chief financial officer/licensing/acquisition/strategic planning]

Fortune 500

- Micron Technology [program/change/performance/quality mgt/strategy/R&D operations]
- Rolls-Royce [Joint Strike Fighter program management/cost reduction]
- AgustaWestlandBell [Presidential helicopter contract, risk management]
- General Electric Energy [six sigma program management/automation/off-shoring]
- General Electric Aircraft Engines [Joint Turbine Advanced Gas Generator - classified U.S. Army program]
- Boeing Commercial Aircraft [Boeing 717 program management]
- Hamilton Sundstrand [product development/joint ventures]
- Toshiba Business Solutions [business process re-engineering]
- Electronic Data Systems (EDS) [management consulting/technical sales]

Government Agencies

- NASA's Engineering and Safety Center [agency-wide communications strategy]
- NASA's Academy of Program, Project and Engineering Leadership [agency-wide strategic and operations plan]
- Naval Electronics Systems Command [program management]

In addition to accumulating practical experience in a wide variety of challenging environments, Mr. Maculley makes an effort to stay current on the latest management theories and research. Some of his formal education includes the following:

- MBA degree in finance and operations graduate, The College of William and Mary, Williamsburg, Virginia, USA
- BSBA degree with Distinction in Marketing graduate, San Diego State University, San Diego, California, USA
- Project Management Professional (PMP) certification, The Project Management Institute, Newtown Square, Pennsylvania, USA
- Six Sigma certification, General Electric Corporation
- John F. Welch (Crotonville) Leadership Development Program graduate, General Electric Corporation

For more information visit www.johnmaculley.com

Index

A

B

C

D

K

L

M

N

O

P

Q

R

S

T

U

V

W

Y

Made in the USA